More VOICES

In Memory of
Hedwig (Hedy) Sorge
Placed by
Carol & Rae Allen

MORE VOICES

UNITED CHURCH PUBLISHING HOUSE

WOOD LAKE PUBLISHING INC

More Voices
Supplement to *Voices United: The Hymn and Worship Book of The United Church of Canada*
Copyright © 2007 The United Church of Canada
L'Église Unie du Canada

All rights reserved. No part of this book may be photocopied, reproduced, or stored in a retrieval system, or transmitted in any form or by any means electronic, mechanical, or otherwise, without the written permission of Wood Lake Publishing Inc.

Copyright is a justice issue. Every effort has been made to find copyright holders for all songs in *More Voices,* and if errors have been made please contact the publisher and corrections will be made and royalties paid for future printings. In some cases authors and composers were found for music previously published as public domain. For traditional songs for which no author or composer could be found we have endeavoured to model a new approach to copyright, one which is contrary to common practice in the publishing industry. We have created new arrangements and translations or paraphrases as necessary for these songs, copyrighting them in the name of The United Church of Canada for protection purposes, and royalties for these arrangements, translations, and paraphrases will be distributed to partner organizations in the countries of origin. In this way we can hopefully break the cycle of powerful organizations, corporations, and individuals making money from the collective intellectual and artistic expressions of indigenous cultures around the world.

Library and Archives Canada Cataloguing in Publication
  More voices [music].
Co-published with Wood Lake Publishing
Includes indexes.
ISBN-13: 978-1-55134-148-4

  1. Hymns, English. 2. United Church of Canada–Hymns.
I. United Church of Canada
M2133.M835 2007   782.27'171792   C2006-905509-2

United Church Publishing House
3250 Bloor St. West, Suite 300
Toronto, Ontario, Canada
M8X 2Y4
bookpub@united-church.ca
www.united-church.ca

Wood Lake Publishing Inc.
9590 Jim Bailey Road
Kelowna, British Columbia, Canada
V4V 1R2
info@woodlakebooks.com
www.woodlakebooks.com

www.morevoices.ca

07   08   09   10   11   5   4   3   2   1

Printed in Canada ✪

Contents

Introduction .... page 6

Acknowledgements .... page 7

Songs listed by song number

    Gathering, Centring, and Invocation 1–25

    Praise 26–63

    Confession, Lament, and Healing 64–86

    Assurance 87–107

    Word 108–134

    Response 135–180

    Offering and Thanksgiving 181–191

    Communion 192–208

    Going Forth 209–225

Indexes

    Copyright Holders .... page 270

    Sources for Hymns and Songs .... page 272

    Scriptural References .... page 274

    Liturgical Use, Topics, and Categories .... page 278

    First Lines and Titles .... page 286

Introduction

Welcome to *More Voices*! Within these pages you will find 225 songs chosen from among the hundreds of pieces that the *More Voices* development team sang together, prayed over, and considered for inclusion. You will also find indexes to enable you to explore the richness and depth of the collection.

Why *More Voices*? When The United Church of Canada's hymn book, *Voices United*, was released in 1996, it became a beloved resource throughout the church. Many congregations are still just discovering the depths of its riches. The past decade, however, has seen a wonderful explosion of new songs of the faith, some created by names well known to us, and others from new composers and poets. At the same time, Christian congregations are expanding their understanding of the kinds of instruments and the types of songs that can help to shape and deepen our worship and faithful living. We are also becoming increasingly attuned to the music of our sisters and brothers throughout the global village, and more profoundly aware than ever of the intertwining of faith with every aspect of our lives on this beautiful, fragile planet.

The time is ripe, then, to continue on the path prepared by *Voices United*, and to enhance our musical lives with, well, *More!* The goal of this supplement is to further enable faith communities to unite in relevant and uplifting congregational song. You will find here more of the voices the church has come to love; more of the theologically balanced, refreshing, and inspirational music that congregations want to sing. But you will also discover in this collection more diversity: more styles, more genres, and more liturgically special music. You will see global and contemporary Christian music alongside a large Canadian and Euro-American repertoire. You will experience tunes, rhythms, and lyrics that may delight you and challenge you. Some of them will ask you to break with familiar church instruments; some will ask you to push the edges of your faith; some will ask you to imagine new places for music in your worshipping life. To assist you in opening up the songs within, we encourage you to visit the *More Voices* website, www.morevoices.ca, which provides additional information about the songs, answers to frequently asked questions, and an opportunity to share the joys and challenges of using this music in your faith communities.

It has been a privilege for those of us on the development team to work with this amazing feast of faith songs. We hope *More Voices* will offer you a taste of the abundance we have encountered and will whet your appetite for *More* to come…

Do sing lustily and with good courage!

Sandra Beardsall
Alan Whitmore
Co-Chairs

Acknowledgements

For the past two and one-half years, I have essentially lived and breathed *More Voices*! What a challenge it has been. It has also been a real blessing to me and a humbling experience to have followed in the footsteps of those who have gone before me in editing song collections for our church.

There are many people to thank, people who shared their gifts and made this book possible. First and foremost, there is the development team, our wonderful team of volunteers from across the country:

Sandra Beardsall (co-chair)	Lynn Boothroyd
Gerri Butler	Rick Gunn
Bill Kervin	Lloyd MacLean
Todd McDonald	Cindy Watson
Alan Whitmore (co-chair)	Sid Woolfrey

These volunteers gave countless hours of their time choosing repertoire through an amazing consensus process and guiding the creation of the liturgical/thematic index, always keeping in mind the overall need for balance in the collection and the ways in which each song could enhance our worship lives. In addition to our volunteers, there were key staff people who walked with us through this process and functioned as full team members: Mark MacLean (liaison, The United Church of Canada); Patti Rodgers (administrative, moral, and musical support) and Michael Schwartzentruber (liaison, Wood Lake Publishing).

The many congregations across Canada and abroad who tested material for us during the summer of 2005 were a blessing to us as we made final decisions regarding content. Your feedback was essential!

Bill Richards from the College of Emmanuel and St. Chad, Saskatoon, organized and compiled our scripture index, incorporating his own suggestions with those of fellow scripture scholars from St. Andrew's College, Saskatoon, and Queen's Theological College, Kingston: David Jobling, Christine Mitchell, and William Morrow. Their collective knowledge of scripture has created an invaluable aid to worship planners.

Alan Whitmore typeset the music for the book, Dianne Greenslade proofread for us, Brenda Allingham acquired copyright permissions, and Margaret Kyle and Kathy Carlisle handled layout. Their patience and skill were much appreciated.

Margaret Kyle also created the wonderful cover art for *More Voices,* an incredible gift to us and to the church.

Finally, we could not have put this book together without the support of management, production, administrative and marketing staff at both The United Church of Canada and Wood Lake Publishing. Many, many thanks to the talented, dedicated staff of both organizations.

To God be the glory!

Bruce Harding
Managing Editor

1 Let Us Build a House
(All Are Welcome)

1 Let us build a house where love can dwell and
2 Let us build a house where proph - ets speak, and
3 Let us build a house where love is found in
4 Let us build a house where hands will reach be -
5 Let us build a house where all are named, their

all can safe - ly live, a place where saints and
words are strong and true, where all God's chil - dren
wa - ter, wine and wheat; a ban - quet hall on
yond the wood and stone to heal and strength - en,
songs and vi - sions heard and loved and treas - ured,

chil - dren tell how hearts learn to for - give. Built of
dare to seek to dream God's reign a - new. Here the
ho - ly ground, where peace and jus - tice meet. Here the
serve and teach, and live the Word they've known. Here the
taught and claimed as words with - in the Word. Built of

Words and music: Marty Haugen; French trans. David Fines, 2006
Words and music copyright © 1994 by GIA Publications, Inc. All rights reserved. 7404 S. Mason Ave., Chicago, IL 60638.
www.giamusic.com. 800-442-1358. Used by permission.
French translation copyright © 2006 by David Fines. Used by permission.

TWO OAKS
Irregular

See next page for French translation.

French translation for *Let Us Build a House*, #1:

1. Bâ-tis-sons un lieu d'a-mour, de foi,
   de par-don, de bon-té,
   où les pe-tits en-fants sont rois
   par leur sim-pli-ci-té.
   Lieu de rê-ves, lieu de vi-sions,
   lieu de grâ-ce pour nous tous,
   où Jé-sus met-tra fin aux di-vi-sions.
   Ve-nez, en-trez! Ve-nez, en-trez!
   Ve-nez, en-trez! C'est chez vous!

2. Bâ-tis-sons un lieu où par-le-ront
   li-bre-ment les pro-phètes;
   les en-fants de Dieu rê-ve-ront
   d'u-ne nou-vel-le Fête.
   U-ne croix se-ra le té-moin
   de la grâ-ce par-mi nous:
   nous se-rons u-nis par l'a-mour di-vin!
   Ve-nez, en-trez! Ve-nez, en-trez!
   Ve-nez, en-trez! C'est chez vous!

3. Bâ-tis-sons un lieu où l'a-mour vient,
   dans l'eau, le vin, le blé;
   un ban-quet dans un mo-ment saint
   de jus-tice et de paix.
   De Dieu l'a-mour s'est ré-vé-lé
   en ce pré-cieux ren-dez-vous :
   le don par-ta-gé de la li-ber-té.
   Ve-nez, en-trez! Ve-nez, en-trez!
   Ve-nez, en-trez! C'est chez vous!

4. Bâ-tis-sons un lieu du-quel nos mains
   s'of-fri-ront en s'ou-vrant,
   pour ser-vir au loin les pro-chains
   au Nom du Dieu vi-vant.
   Ceux qui sont cour-bés, op-pri-més,
   en-fin se met-tront de-bout;
   les dan-gers et leurs peurs sont é-car-tés.
   Ve-nez, en-trez! Ve-nez, en-trez!
   Ve-nez, en-trez! C'est chez vous!

5. Bâ-tis-sons un lieu d'hu-ma-ni-té,
   de paix, de com-mu-nion,
   cha-cun ac-cueil-li, ac-cep-té
   ap-pe-lé par son nom,
   s'y mê-lant les pleurs et la joie,
   et les chants fer-vents et doux.
   En ce lieu, par-tout, chan-te-ront
      nos voix:
   Ve-nez, en-trez! Ve-nez, en-trez!
   Ve-nez, en-trez! C'est chez vous!

2   Come All You People
(Uyai mose)

* alternative: "your God"

Enjoy this song as written or make up your own harmonies.
Shona pronunciation: *Oo-yah-ee moh-say, tee-nah-mah-tay mwah-ree, oo-yah-ee moh-say zvee-noh.*

Words: Alexander Gondo, Zimbabwe; English paraphrase: I-to Loh
Music: Alexander Gondo, Zimbabwe, notated by I-to Loh; Arrangement: John L. Bell, 1995
Words, music and English paraphrase copyright © 1986 World Council of Churches. Used by permission.
Arrangement copyright © 1995 by WGRG, Iona Community, Scotland, admin. GIA Publications, Inc., excl. N. American agent. All rights reserved.
Used by permission.

3

River
(Rivière)

Unison
♩ = 120

Repeat three times

1 Ri - ver,   rush-a-down to the
2 Spir - it,   come-a-down to the
3 Wa - ter,   let me drink of your
4 Ri - ver,   flow-a-down where you

o - cean blue,   Ri - ver
ri - ver - side,   Spir - it,
hea - ling pow'r,   Wa - ter,
ran be - fore,   Ri - ver,

from   a moun - tain high.
spark of won - drous thought.
strength and life you give.
source of clear - er view.

Words and music: Julian Pattison, 2003; French trans. David Fines, 2006

Words and music copyright © 2003 Julian Pattison. All rights reserved. 2593 7th Ave. East, Vancouver, BC. (604) 817-5728. www.eaglewingmusic.org.
Used by permission.

French translation copyright © 2006 David Fines. Used by permission.

Ri - ver, as you do what ri - vers do,
Spir - it, I am free for you to guide,
Wa - ter, as I tra - vel with each hour,
Ri - ver, as I walk your rock - y shore,

Ri - ver, draw the Spir - it nigh.
Spir - it, pray that I be taught!
Wa - ter, help my bo - dy live.
Ri - ver, see my jour - ney through.

Repeat three times

See my jour - ney through.

French:

1. Ri-vière, cou-le, cou-le vers l'o-céan,
   Ri-vière, par monts et prai-ries,
   Ri-vière, comme il se doit,
     dou-ce-ment;
   Ri-vière, par toi, vient l'Es-prit.

2. Es-prit, cou-le, cou-le près de la rive,
   Es-prit, cou-rant mer-veil-leux;
   Es-prit, ta fraî-cheur guide et ra-vive,
   Esprit, ou-vre-moi les yeux!

3. Eau vive, a-breu-ve-moi et gué-ris-moi;
   Eau vive, ma force et ma vie;
   Eau vive, sur les sen-tiers de ma foi,
   Eau vive, tu m'é-pa-nou-is.

4. Ri-vière, cou-le, cou-le les mê-mes
     cours,
   Ri-vière, ou-vre des pas-sages;
   Ri-vière, tout au long de
     mon par-cours,

4 All Who Are Thirsty

All who are thirs - ty,
all who are weak, come to the foun - tain.
Dip your heart in the stream of life. Let the pain and the sor-
row be washed a - way in the waves of his

Words and music: Benton Brown and Glenn Robertson, 1998
Words and music copyright © 1998 Vineyard Songs (UK/Eire) (admin. In North America by Music Services, o/b/o Vineyard Music Global, Inc.)
All rights reserved. Used by permission.

5 Holy Spirit, You're Like the Wind
(Sheng ling ru feng)

Mandarin:
1 Sheng ling ru feng, feng he ru? Dan wen
(translit.) 2 Sheng ling ru chuan ching shan lu, huo zuo
3 Sheng ling ru yu chang jiao zhu, yu man

English:
1 Ho - ly Spir - it, you're like the wind, blow - ing
2 Ho - ly Spir - it, you're like a spring, flow - ing
3 Ho - ly Spir - it, you're like the oil that lights

feng sheng zhi tou guo, feng guo zhi tou hao hua
qi liu huo fei bao, huo zuo chiang he yu' yu
deng chan kuang man wu, yu cuo gao hu man yi

gent - ly a - bove the trees; where the wind blows, the flow-ers
o'er moun-tain or a fall, like a riv - er that flows with
hous - es with glow-ing lamps; you're like oint-ment poured out in

kai, sheng ming hua kai feng choi chu, chang chui
chi, huo shui zhi yün, shu chang lu. Zhi yün
chin, sheng ai xing xiang xiang fu you, chang ciao

bloom, where the wind blows there is life. May it
power, there to nour - ish the trees and fields. May you
love, like God's love which fills my heart. O a -

Words and music: Wei-fan Wang, China
English trans. Grace Shangjuan, Ivy Balchin and W. H. Wong, alt.
Arrangement: Gou-ren Zhong
Words, music, arrangement and English translation copyright © 1983, 1999 China Christian Council. All rights reserved. Used by permission.
Mandarin translit copyright © 2004 General Board of Global Ministries, GBGMusik, 475 Riverside Dr., New York, NY 10115. All rights reserved.
Used by permission.

6 Holy Spirit, Come into Our Lives

Unison *Ostinato Refrain*

Ho - ly Spir - it, come in-to our lives.

Ho - ly Spir - it, make us tru - ly wise.

Verses

1 Give us a spir - it of wis - dom, an
2 Give us a spir - it of cour - age, and
3 Spir - it of love and com-pas - sion, give
4 Spir - it of all con-so - la - tion, O
5 Spir - it of light and of wis - dom, O
6 Spir - it of strength and of heal - ing, bend

un - der - stand - ing heart. Give us a spir - it of knowl -
judg-ment that is wise. Give us a spir - it of rev -
hope to all the poor. Spir - it of jus - tice and mer -
lift our hearts this day. Spir - it of all un - der - stand -
lift us from our sor - row. Spir - it of peace and for - give -
stub - born hearts and will. Spir - it of trust and of car -

This versatile song can be sung in a number of ways. The refrain may be sung on its own as a simple chant or alternating with the verses, or it can be sung as an ostinato with the solo verses sung over top as the Spirit moves. The verses are best sung by a soloist or choir with the congregation singing the refrain.

Words and music: Ken Canedo, 1998
Words and music copyright © 1998 by Ken Canedo. Published by OCP Publications. All rights reserved. Used with permission.

edge, and lead us to the truth.
'rence, of won-der and of awe.
cy, come o-pen ev - 'ry door.
ing, O help us know your way.
ness, O help us face to - mor - row.
ing, O melt us, warm our chill.

Gather Us In

7

(Rassemble-nous)

Ga - ther us in, ground us in you. Ga - ther us
in, ground us in you. Ga - ther us in, ga - ther us
in, ground us, ground us in you.

French:
Ras-sem-ble-nous, tout près de toi.
Ras-sem-ble-nous, tout près de toi.
Ras-sem-ble-nous, ras-sem-ble-nous,
tout près, tout près de toi.

A centring song, for gathering and rooting ourselves in God.

Words and music: David Hann, 2005; French trans. David Fines, 2006
Words and music copyright © 2005 David Hann. Used by permission.
French translation copyright © 2006. David Fines. Used by permission.

8

And on This Path

A gospel-flavoured setting of Psalm 118:19.

Words: Lynn Bauman Music: Linnea Good, 2003
Words copyright © 2000 Lynn Bauman, from *Ancient Songs Sung Anew: the Psalms as Poetry.* Used by permission.
Music copyright © 2003 Borealis Music, www.LinneaGood.com. Used by permission.

Venite, Exultemus Domino

(O Come and Let Us Sing)

9

Latin: Ve - ni - te, e - xul - te - mus Do - mi - no, ve -
English: O come and let us sing to God, our hope, God's

ni - te, a - do - re - mus. Ve - ni - te, e - xul - te - mus
mer - cy is for ev - er. O come and let us sing to

Do - mi - no, ve - ni - te, a - do - re - mus.
God, our hope. God's mer - cy is for ev - er.

A versatile song for gathering, assurance of pardon, and general use.

Words and music: Taizé Community
Words and music copyright © 1982, 1991, Taizé Community, France, admin. GIA Publications, Inc., excl. N. American agent. All rights reserved. Used by permission.

10 Come and Seek the Ways of Wisdom

A hymn which seeks to express a trinitarian theology based on scriptural Wisdom images.

Words: Ruth Duck, 1993
Music: Donna Kasbohm, 1995
Words copyright © 1996 and music copyright © 1997 The Pilgrim Press. Used by permission.

MADELEINE
878787
Alternate tune: PICARDY

Come, Come Emmanuel

11

This gentle chant works well with or without the cantor's part. There are two independent sets of words for a cantor: verses 1-6 are words for Advent or times of invocation; the words for the Kyrie ("Lord, have mercy...") below are for prayers of confession and similar occasions.

Words and music: James J. Chepponis, 1995
Words, music and arrangement copyright © 1995 by GIA Publications, Inc. All rights reserved. 7404 S. Mason Ave., Chicago, IL 60638.
www.giamusic.com. 800-442-1358. Used by permission.

12 Come Touch Our Hearts
(Come Touch and Bless)

1 Come touch our hearts that we may know com - pas - sion,
2 Come touch our souls that we may know and love you,
3 Come touch our minds and teach us how to rea - son,
4 Come touch us in the mo - ments we are fra - gile,
5 Come touch us now, this peo - ple who are ga - thered,

from fail - ing em - bers build a blaz - ing fire;
your qui - et pre - sence all our fears dis - pel;
set free our thoughts to won - der and to dream;
and in our weak - ness your great strength re - veal;
to break the bread and share the cup of peace;

love strong e - nough to o - ver - turn in - jus - tice, to
cre - ate a space for spir - it to grow in us, let
help us to o - pen doors of un - der - stand - ing, to
that we may rise to fol - low and to serve,
that we may love you with our heart, our soul, our

seek a world more gra - cious, come touch and bless our hearts.
life and beau - ty fill us, come touch and bless our souls.
wel - come truth and wis - dom, come touch and bless our minds.
stea - dy now our nerve, come touch and bless our wills.
mind, our strength, our all, come touch us with your grace.

Words and music: Gordon Light, 2002; arr. Andrew Donaldson, 2002
Words and music copyright © 2002 Common Cup Company, www.commoncup.com. Used by permission.
Arrangement copyright © 2002 by Andrew Donaldson. Used by permission.

O Let the Power Fall on Me

1 O let the pow-er fall on me, my Lord*, let the
2 For we want jus-tice and truth and love, my Lord*, we want

pow-er fall on me; O let the pow-er from heav-en
jus-tice and truth and love; for we want jus-tice and truth and

fall on me, let the pow-er fall on me.
love, my Lord*, we want jus-tice and truth and love.

* alternative: "my God"

This song of invocation should be accompanied in a reggae style, accenting the eighth-note offbeat, for example:

simile

Words (verse one): Birchfield Aymer; words (verse two): Author unknown
Music: traditional song, Caribbean, adapted by Birchfield Aymer; arr. Patrick Prescod
Words and music copyright © The Caribbean Conference of Churches. Used by permission.

14 Where Two or Three Are Gathered

Where two or three are ga-thered in my name, I am
there, I am there.

Words and music: Bruce Harding, 2002, after Matthew 18:20.
Words and music copyright © 2002 by Bruce Harding, www.evensong.ca. Used by permission.

15 Holy Sacred Spirit

Ho - ly sa - cred Spir - it, breathe your breath on us.

Cre - ate a new heart in me, oh God, en -
Send forth your Spirit and re - new the earth, the

Ho - ly sa - cred Spir - it,

flame my heart with your love, your Spi - rit of love.
long - ing earth, the wait - ing earth, the fra - gile earth.

breathe your life in us.

Try this gentle chant with or without the soloist's part above.

Words and music: Monica Brown, 1991
Words and music copyright © 1991 Monica Brown & Emmaus Productions. Used by permission.

Confitemini Domino

16

(Come and Fill Our Hearts)

Latin: Con - fi - te - mi - ni Do - mi - no quo - ni - am bo - nus.
English: Come and fill our hearts with your peace. You a - lone, O Lord*, are ho - ly.

Con - fi - te - mi - ni Do - mi - no, al - le - lu - ia!
Come and fill our hearts with your peace, al - le - lu - ia!

* alternative: "O God"

A shorter song for gathering, centring, and healing prayer.

Words: Taizé Community, 1982
Music: Jacques Berthier, 1982
Words and music copyright © 1982, 1991, Taizé Community, France, admin. GIA Publications, Inc., excl. N. American agent. All rights reserved.
Used by permission.

17 God in the Darkness

1 God in the dark - ness, God be - yond our know - ing, pa - tient cre-
2 God in the dark - ness, God in all our griev - ing, friend of our
3 God in the dark - ness, God of ho - ly dream - ing, gi - ver of

a - tor, seed in se - cret grow - ing, rock of the liv - ing,
tears, com - pan - ion ne - ver leav - ing, draw - ing us past the
hope, and pledge of our re - deem - ing, Spir - it of truth, our

wa - ter e - ver flow - ing, come and re - new us.
li - mits of be - liev - ing, come and re - new us.
mem - or - y and mean - ing, come and re - new us.

Words: Elizabeth J. Smith, 1998
Music: Colin Gibson, 1998
Words copyright © Elizabeth J. Smith (624 Centre Rd., Bentleigh East 3165 Australia. ejsmith@pacific.net.au)
Music copyright © 1998 Hope Publishing Company, Carol Stream, IL 60188. All rights reserved. Used by permission.

TRARALGON
11 11 11 5
Alternate tune: ISTE CONFESSOR

18 Lord, Prepare Me to Be a Sanctuary

Lord*, pre - pare me to be a sanc - tu - ar - y, pure and

ho - ly tried and true; with thanks - giv - ing, I'll be a

liv - ing sanc-tu - ar - y for you.

* alternative: "God"

A song for gathering, baptism, and other times of preparation.

Words and music: John W. Thompson and Randy Scruggs

Words and music copyright © 1982 for all territories of the world by Whole Armour & Full Armor Publishing Companies. Administered for the World by The Kruger Organisation, Inc. International Copyright Secured – All rights reserved – Used by permission.

Maranatha 19

English: Ma-ra - na-tha, ma-ra - na-tha, come, Lord Je - sus, come. Ma-ra-
French: *Ma-ra - na-tha, ma-ra - na-tha, viens, Jé - sus Christ. Ma-ra-*

na - tha, ma-ra - na - tha, come, Lord Je - sus, come.
na - tha, ma-ra - na - tha, viens, Jé - sus Christ.

"Maranatha" is an Aramaic word meaning "Come, Lord."

Words: traditional liturgical text; French trans. *More Voices*, 2007
Music: Louise Skibsted
Music copyright © Louise Skibsted. Used by permission.

20 God of Still Waiting

1 God of still wait - ing, God of deep long - ing, God of the
2 Spir - it of prom - ise, Spir - it of pur - pose, Spir - it of
3 Word who comes to us, Word who lives with us, Word who dis -
4 Word true and faith - ful, hope-bring-ing Spir - it, God of en -

heart's true rest: hold us in fath - om - less peace,
cease - less prayer: bathe us in life full and free,
turbs and heals: si - lence our chat - ter - ing fears,
fold - ing love: come in your full - ness and grace; (guard)

guard us with un - wan - ing love.
kin - dle our won - der and hope.
wak - en our un - con - scious faith.
work through our lives for your praise.

Words: Carl P. Daw, Jr., 2000
Music: Alfred V. Fedak, 2000

HESYCHIA
5 5 6 7 7

Words copyright © 2000 Hope Publishing Company, Carol Stream, IL 60188. All rights reserved. Used by permission.
Music copyright © 2001 Selah Publishing Co. Inc. www.selahpub.com. All rights reserved. Used by permission.

Open Our Hearts

(Ouvre nos cœurs)

A song for centring and discernment.

Words and music: Jim Strathdee; French trans. David Fines, 2006
Words and music copyright © Jim and Jean Strathdee (Desert Flower Music), PO Box 1476, Carmichael, CA 95609l (916) 481-2999.
www.strathdeemusic.com. Used by permission.
French translation copyright © 2006 David Fines. Used by permission.

22 # God of All the World
(Mi pela i bung)

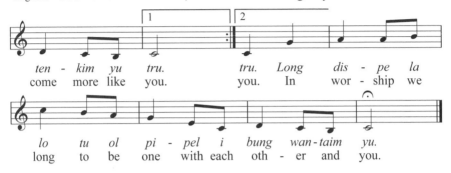

♩ = 86

Tok Pisin: *Mi pe-la i bung pa-pa God long on-rim yu na long*
English: God of all the world, we have come to give you thanks and be-

1. ten - kim yu tru. **2.** tru. Long dis - pe la
come more like you. you. In wor - ship we

lo tu ol pi - pel i bung wan - taim yu.
long to be one with each oth - er and you.

Drum

simile

Words: traditional song, Papua New Guinea; English trans. Fred Kaan
Music: traditional song, Papua New Guinea, transcribed by I-to Loh

English translation copyright © 1991 Hope Publishing Company, Carol Stream, IL 60188. All rights reserved. Used by permission.
Music copyright © 1991 by I-to Loh. Used by permission.

French translation for *Come, O Holy Spirit*, #23:

1. Saint-Es-prit, viens, oh, viens, sai-sis
   ton É-glise,
   En la frap-pant d'é-clairs, que tu
   la con-dui-ses.
   Con-su-me nos lour-deurs,
   no-tre su-per-flu,
   Nos sa-crées cou-tu-mes, au nom
   de Jé-sus.

   Refrain:
   Viens, viens, au nom de Jé-sus,
   Tem-pête en nos cœurs;
   Par-tout c'est l'at-ten-te
   La Pente-côte est là!
   Et je dis:
   Viens, viens, au nom de Jé-sus,
   Tem-pête en nos cœurs;
   Par-tout c'est l'at-ten-te
   La Pente-côte est là!

2. Viens dé-fai-re les nœuds de nos
   cer-ti-tudes;
   Viens, ba-laie au loin nos vieil-les
   ha-bi-tu-des.
   Vent nou-veau, souffle en nous,
   se-coue nos tor-peurs;
   In-suf-fle-nous l'a-mour, tem-pête
   en nos cœurs...

3. Viens et li-bè-re-nous de nos
   ba-bil-lages,
   Et que chan-tent nos voix d'un
   com-mun lan-ga-ge.
   Il-lu-mi-ne nos vies, rem-plis-nous
   de foi;
   Par-tout c'est l'at-ten-te: La Pente-côte
   est là!

   ...A-men

Come, O Holy Spirit
(Wind of Change)

23

1 Come, O Ho-ly Spir-it, set the Church on
2 Blow a-way the cob-webs of our stub-born
3 Free us from the bab-ble of our Ba-bel

fire; strike it as the light-ning
past. Come, send fly-ing from us
mind; spark in us a lan-guage

hits a pos-ing spire. Burn a-way the
myths un-fit to last. Wind of change, re-
all can un-der-stand. Light-en then our

struc-tures and con-sume the sham
fresh us and dis-turb our calm;
dark-ness, come and show us how

Words: Fred Kaan, 1972, rev. 1998; French trans. David Fines, 2006
Music: Ron Klusmeier, 2000

Words copyright © 1972, 1998 Hope Publishing Company, Carol Stream, IL 60188. All rights reserved. Used by permission.
Music copyright © 2000 by Ron Klusmeier, www.musiklus.com. Used by permission.
French translation copyright © 2006 by David Fines. Used by permission.

24 Breath of God, Breath of Peace

Unison
♩ = 72

1 Breath of God, Breath of peace, Breath of love, Breath of life, Breath of
2 Word of God, Word of peace, Word of love, Word of life, Word of
3 Voice of God, Voice of peace, Voice of love, Voice of life, Voice of

jus-tice, Breath of pas-sion, Breath cre - a-ting, Breath of heal - ing,
jus-tice, Word of pas-sion, Word cre - a-ting, Word of heal - ing,
jus-tice, Voice of pas-sion, Voice cre - a-ting, Voice of heal - ing,

Breath of sing-ing, Breath of pray-ing, come u - pon us, come re-
Word of sing-ing, Word of pray-ing, come u - pon us, come re-
Voice of sing-ing, Voice of pray-ing, come u - pon us, come re-

store us, come in - spire us, Breath of God.
store us, come in - spire us, Word of God.
store us, come in - spire us, Voice of God.

Words: Adam M.L. Tice, 2004
Music: Fred Kimball Graham, 2006

EMMANUEL COLLEGE
irregular

Words copyright © 2004 by Adam M.L. Tice, Goshen, IN, USA. amltice@yahoo.com. Used by permission.
Music copyright © 2006 Emmanuel College, Toronto. (Emmanuel College, 75 Queen's Park Cres, Toronto, ON M5S 1K7). ec@utoronto.ca. Used by permission.

O God, Send Out Your Spirit

25

pain and the tears, your Spir-it em-pow-ers us and

Spir-it-filled tune; Love says, "Re-mem-ber why we

soon we face our fears.

do the things we do."

Verse 3

3 Ev-'ry time a per-son reach-ing out

A lively setting of Psalm 104.

Words (refrain): The International Commission on English in the Liturgy (ICEL)
Words (verses) and music: Jesse Manibusan, 1996
Music and verse text copyright © 1996 Jesse Manibusan. Published by spiritandsong.com ®. All rights reserved. Used with permission.
Refrain text copyright © ICEL. All rights reserved.

26

Your Love Is Amazing
(Hallelujah)

1,3 Your love is a - maz - ing, stea - dy and un - changing, I can feel it ris-

ing, your love is a moun - tain, firm be - neath my feet.
ing, all the joy that's grow - ing deep in - side of me.

Your love is a mys - t'ry, how you gent - ly lift
Ev -'ry time I see you all your good - ness shines

Words and music: Brenton Brown and Brian Doerksen
Words and music copyright © 2000 Vineyard Songs (UK/EIRE). Admin in North America by Music Services o/b/o Vineyard Music Global Inc. (PRS).
Used by permission.

jah,   hal - le - lu - jah,

your love makes me sing.

2 Your love is   sur-pris-
3 Your love is   a - maz-

Hal - le - lu - jah.

27   Creator God You Gave Us Life

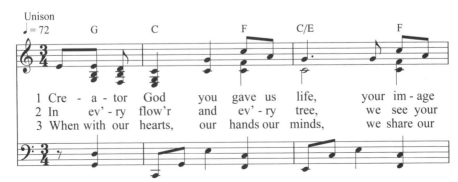

1 Cre - a - tor   God   you   gave us   life,   your im - age
2 In   ev' - ry   flow'r   and   ev' - ry   tree,   we see your
3 When with our   hearts,   our   hands our   minds,   we share our

Words and music: Judith Snowdon, 2004
Words and music copyright © 2004 by Judith Snowdon. Used by permission.

CLAIRE
8 8 8 8 D
Alternate tune: CANDLER

28

God of the Bible
(Fresh as the Morning)

Unison
♩. = 54

1 God of the Bi - ble, God in the Gos - pel,
2 God in our strug - gles, God in our hun - ger,
♦ 3 Those with - out sta - tus, those who are noth - ing,
4 Not by your fin - ger, not by your an - ger
5 Hope we must car - ry, shin - ing and cer - tain

hope seen in Je - sus, hope yet to come,
suf - fer - ing with us, tak - ing our part,
♦ you have made roy - al, gift - ed with rights,
will our world or - der change in a day,
through all our tur - moil, ter - ror and loss,

you are our cen - tre, day - light or dark - ness,
still you em - pow'r us, moth - er - ing Spir - it,
♦ cho - sen as part - ners, mid - wives of jus - tice,
but by your peo - ple, fear - less and faith - ful,
bond - ing us glad - ly one to the oth - er,

Words: Shirley Erena Murray, 1995
Music: Tony E. Alonso, 2001
Words copyright © 1996 Hope Publishing Company, Carol Stream, IL 60188. All rights reserved. Used by permission.
Music copyright © 2001 by GIA Publications, Inc. All rights reserved. 7404 S. Mason Ave., Chicago, IL 60638.
www.giamusic.com. 800-442-1358. Used by permission.

29 How Lovely Is Your Dwelling Place

* alternative: "O God"

A song of joy in the presence of God, from Psalm 82:2–11.

Words and music: Matt Redman, 1995
Words and music copyright © 1995 Thankyou Music (PRS), administered by EMI CMG Publishing, excluding Europe, which is administered by kingswaysong.com.
Used by permission.

30   It's a Song of Praise to the Maker

1 It's a song of praise to the Mak - er, the
2 It's a call of life to the Giv - er when
3 It's a hymn of love to the Lov - er; the
4 It's the chor - us of all cre - a - tion; it's

thrush sings high in the tree. It's a song of praise to the
waves and wat-er-falls roar. It's a call of life to the
bum - ble-bees hum a - long. It's a hymn of love to the
sung by all liv ing things. It's the chor - us of all cre-

Mak - er, the gray whale sings in the sea,
Giv - er when high tides break on the shore,
Lov - er; the sum - mer breeze joins the song,
a - tion; a song the u - ni - verse sings,

Words: Ruth Duck, 1992
Music: Ron Klusmeier, 1992
Words copyright © 1992 by GIA Publications, Inc. All rights reserved. 7404 S. Mason Ave., Chicago, IL 60638. www.giamusic.com. 800-442-1358.
Music copyright © 1992 by Ron Klusmeier, www.musiklus.com. Used by permission.

31 Pure Love

Pure love, pure truth,
Pure love, pure truth,
pure jus - tice, God.
pure jus - tice, God.

Try this song with two groups singing antiphonally, coming together on the last word, "God."

Words: Lynn Bauman and Linnea Good.   Music: Linnea Good, 2003
Words from the poetry of Lynn Bauman, copyright © Lynn Bauman. Used by permission.
Music copyright © 2003 Borealis Music, www.LinneaGood.com. Used by permission.

32 Hallelujah (Pattison)

Hal - le, hal - le - lu - jah, hal - le, hal - le - lu,

hal - le, hal - le-lu-jah. Hal - le - lu - jah!

Try this song with percussion as notated. Any combination of a lower and higher instrument (wood blocks, congas, etc.) will work well.

Words: traditional liturgical text   Music: Julian Pattison, 2003
Music copyright © 2003 by Julian Pattison. All rights reserved. 2593 7th Ave. East, Vancouver, BC. (604) 817-5728. www.eaglewingmusic.org. Used by permission.

Jesus Came Bringing Us Hope   33

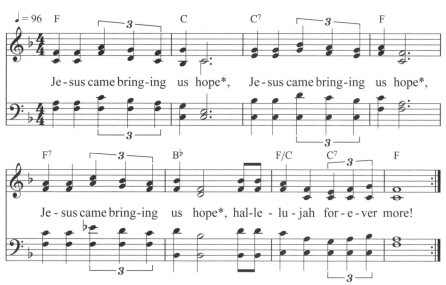

Je - sus came bring-ing us hope*, Je - sus came bring-ing us hope*,

Je - sus came bring-ing us hope*, hal-le - lu - jah for - e - ver more!

* additional verses: "peace," "love," "joy," etc.

The harmonies for this song are only suggestions. Try creating your own harmonies by ear.

Words and music: traditional song, Cameroon; arr. *More Voices*, 2007
Arrangement copyright © 2007 The United Church of Canada.

34 All Is Done for the Glory
(Tout est fait pour la gloire)

Additional verse:

Verse 4 (French): L'of-frande est pour la gloi-re de Dieu...
Verse 4 (English): All is giv'n for the glo-ry of God...

A call and response song from francophone West Africa. Improvise harmonies based on the right hand of the piano.

Words and music: Abel Nkuinji, Cameroon; English translation: S T Kimbrough, Jr.
Words and music copyright © Abel Nkuinji. English translation copyright © 2004 General Board of Global Ministries, GBG Musik, 475 Riverside Dr., New York, NY 10115. All rights reserved. Used by permission.

Holy One, O Holy One

35

A blessing hymn for marriage and commitment.

Words: Walter Farquharson, 1990
Music: Ron Klusmeier, 1992, rev. 1998
Words copyright © 1990 by Walter Farquharson. Used by permission.
Music copyright © 1992 by Ron Klusmeier, www.musiklus.com. Used by permission.

36

Glory to God
(Gloria a Dios)

A call and response song which sings well with lots of percussion and energy.

Words: traditional liturgical text; French trans. David Fines, 2006
Music: traditional melody, Peru; arr. *More Voices*, 2007
French translation copyright © 2006 David Fines. Used by permission. Arrangement copyright © .

Each Blade of Grass

(Circle of God)

1 Each blade of grass, ev'-ry wing that soars, the waves that
2 Each si-lent paw, ev'-ry round-ed stone, the buzz that
3 Each i-cy peak, ev'-ry pat-terned shell, the joy-ous

sweep a-cross a dis-tant shore, make full the cir-cle of God.
ech-oes from a hon-ey'd comb, make full the cir-cle of God.
chor-us that the dawn fore-tells, make full the cir-cle of God.

Each laugh-ing child, ev'-ry gen-tle eye, a for-est
Each fire-brimmed star, ev'-ry out-stretched hand, the wind that
Each cos-mic hue, ev'-ry crea-ture's way, all form the

lit be-neath a moon-bright sky, make full the cir-cle of God.
leaps and sails a-cross the land, make full the cir-cle of God.
beau-ty of this vast ar-ray, mak-ing full the cir-cle of God.

Words: Keri K. Wehlander, 2005.
Music: Anonymous, from *The United States' Sacred Harmony*, 1799, adapted; arrangement: Linnea Good, 2005.
Words copyright © 2005 Keri K. Wehlander, www.creativeworship.ca. Used by permission.
Arrangement copyright © 2005 Borealis Music, www.LinneaGood.com. Used by permission.

RHODE ISLAND
9 10 7 D

38 Glory to God
(Nzamuranza)

* an alternate English paraphrase:

We sing your praise,
Jesus yesterday, today and forever.

Xitswa pronunciation: *Nzah-muh-rahn-zah, ah-ngah-koh-nah wah-koo-fah-nah-nah nah-yay.*

Words and music: traditional Xitswa song, Mozambique
Arrangement: Patrick Matsikenyiri, 2003
English trans. Patrick Matsikenyiri and Dan Damon, 2003; alternate English para. *More Voices*, 2007
English translation and arrangement copyright © 2003 by Patrick Matsikenyiri. All rights reserved. Used by permission.
Alternate English paraphrase copyright © .

Mother Earth, Our Mother Birthing

1 Moth-er Earth, our Moth-er birth-ing
2 Sis-ter Air, our Sis-ter lift-ing
3 Broth-er Wa-ter, Broth-er pul-sing
4 Fath-er Fire, our Fath-er burn-ing

Percussion continues throughout

ev'-ry crea-ture from the ground. Je-sus too was
ev'-ry crea-ture born with wings; Je-sus shared the
deep through ev'-ry vein and sea, Je-sus drank the
with the sac-red urge to live. Je-sus' death com-

flesh and breath-ing, kin to all that's green and brown.
breath of for-ests, breath that makes our spir-its sing.
ver-y rain-drops for our wine and in our tea.
pletes the cy-cle, bring-ing life be-yond the grave.

Cel-e-brate with all cre-a-tion: God has formed the web of life;

Cel-e-brate with all cre-a-tion God has formed the web of life.

Words: Norman Habel, 1999
Music: Neil Weisensel, 2006
Words copyright © 1999 Norman Habel. Administered by Willow Publishing Pty. Ltd. All rights reserved. Used by permission.
Music copyright © 2006 Neil Weisensel. SOCAN. www.neilmusic.com. Used by permission.

MIRACLE
8 7 8 7 8 7
Alternate tune:
REGENT SQUARE

40   Never Ending Joy

Unison *Refrain*

Nev-er end-ing joy, nev-er end-ing joy, nev-er end-ing joy,

nev-er end-ing joy, nev-er end-ing joy, nev-er end-ing joy!

1 God of ev-ery tribe, ev-ery lan-guage, God of ev-ery riv-er and sea,
2 God of ev-ery hill, ev-ery val-ley, God of ev-ery leaf, ev-ery tree,
3 God of ev-ery song, ev-ery sto-ry, God of ev-ery cap-tive set free,

God of ev-ery moun-tain and is-land, you bring joy to me.
God of ev-ery cloud, ev-ery rain-drop, you bring joy to me.
God of ev-ery dance, ev-ery foot-step, you bring joy to me.

Words and music: Daniel Charles Damon, 2003
Words and music copyright © 2006 Hope Publishing Company, Carol Stream, IL 60188. All rights reserved. Used by permission.

HELOBUNG
9 8 9 5 with refrain

O Beautiful Gaia

O beau-ti-ful Gai - a, O Gai - a, call-ing us home.

O beau-ti-ful Gai - a, call - ing us on.

1 Soil yield-ing its har - vest, O Gai - a, call-ing us home.
2 Waves crash-ing on gran - ite, O Gai - a, call-ing us home.
3 Pine bend-ing in wind - storm, O Gai - a, call-ing us home.
4 Loon nest-ing in marsh - land, O Gai - a, call-ing us home.

Soil yield - ing its har - vest,
Waves crash - ing on gran - ite,
Pine bend - ing in wind - storm,
Loon nest - ing in marsh - land,

call - ing us on.

The term Gaia (guy'-ah) represents "Mother Earth," inviting us to live into our care and respect for all creation. It asks us to consider our relationship to the earth in the context of our faith.

Words and music: Carolyn McDade, with verses created by the singers gathered in Atlantic Canada.
Arrangement: Lydia Pedersen, 2006.
Words and music copyright © Carolyn McDade Music. www.gis.net/~surtsey/mcdade. Email: surtsey@gis.net. Used by permission.
Arrangement copyright © 2006 by Lydia Pedersen. Used by permission.

42 Praise God for This Holy Ground

Suitable for use at either the beginning or end of worship, this song offers gratitude for the physical space and identifiable people on which and among whom worship takes place.

Words and music: John L. Bell, 2002
Words and music copyright © 2002 by WGRG, Iona Community, Scotland, admin.
GIA Publications, Inc., excl. N. American agent. All rights reserved. Used by permission.

HEYMONYSTRAAT
7 7 12 7

The Play of the Godhead

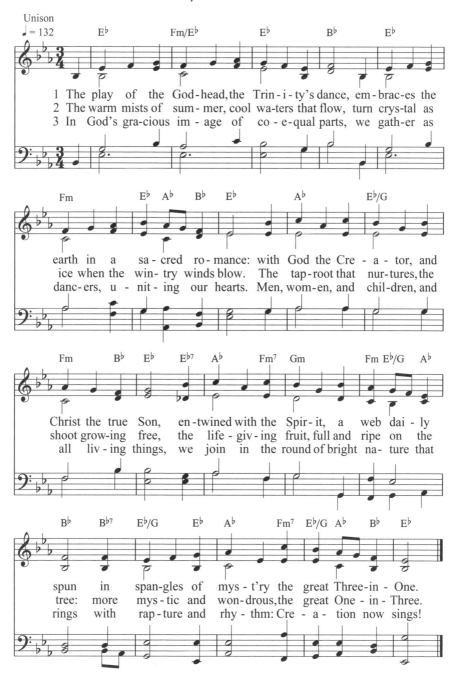

1 The play of the God-head, the Trin-i-ty's dance, em-brac-es the
2 The warm mists of sum-mer, cool wa-ters that flow, turn crys-tal as
3 In God's gra-cious im-age of co-e-qual parts, we gath-er as

earth in a sa-cred ro-mance: with God the Cre-a-tor, and
ice when the win-try winds blow. The tap-root that nur-tures, the
danc-ers, u-nit-ing our hearts. Men, wom-en, and chil-dren, and

Christ the true Son, en-twined with the Spir-it, a web dai-ly
shoot grow-ing free, the life-giv-ing fruit, full and ripe on the
all liv-ing things, we join in the round of bright na-ture that

spun in span-gles of mys-t'ry the great Three-in-One.
tree: more mys-tic and won-drous, the great One-in-Three.
rings with rap-ture and rhy-thm: Cre-a-tion now sings!

Words: Mary Louise Bringle, 2000
Music: Robert J. Batastini, 2003
Words copyright © 2002 and music copyright © 2003 by GIA Publications, Inc.,
7404 S. Mason Ave., Chicago, IL 60638. www.giamusic.com . 800-442-1358. Used by permission.

BEDFORD PARK
11 11 11 11 11

44 Shadow and Substance

1 Shad-ow and sub-stance, won-der and mys-ter-y, spell-bind-ing
2 We are your im-age, formed in com-mu-ni-ty; sis-ters and
3 Nam-ing the name-less Spir-it of u-ni-ty, scan-ning the

spin-ner of at-oms and earth; soul of the cos-mos, per-son and
broth-ers of Ad-am and Eve. You gave us col-our, cus-tom and
heav-ens for signs of your care; God of the a-ges, give us hu-

en-er-gy, source of our be-ing, we sing of your worth.
his-to-ry; teach us to hon-our what oth-ers re-ceive.
mil-i-ty; guide us to mys-ti-cal un-ion in prayer.

Words and music: Daniel Charles Damon, 1989
Words copyright © 1994 and music copyright © 1993 Hope Publishing Company, Carol Stream, IL 60188.
All rights reserved. Used by permission.

TWILIGHT
5 6 10 D

You Are Holy
(Hamba nathi)

* additional English verses: "You are freedom," "You are justice."

*The Zulu text means "Go/Walk/Travel with us, our Liberator." **Zulu pronunciation:** Hahm-bah nah-tee koo-loo-lee weh-too. The English paraphrase attempts to capture the journey essence of the original text while expanding upon the notion of God as "Liberator."*

Words and music: traditional song, South Africa
English paraphrase and arrangement: *More Voices*, 2007
English paraphrase and arrangement copyright © .

46 Bless the Lord

Bless the Lord*, O my soul, bless God's ho-ly name.

Bless the Lord*, O my soul, bless God's ho-ly name.

Bless the Lord*.

1 Re - mem - ber the kind-ness of our God,
2 Re - mem - ber the jus-tice of our God,
3 Re - mem - ber the heal-ing love of God,

* alternative: "Bless our God"

Words and music: Dan Brennan, Marc Cavallero, Kevin Roth and Ken Canedo, 1995
Words and music copyright © 1995, 2002, Ken Canedo, Dan Brennan, Kevin Roth, Marc Cavellero. Published by spiritandsong.com ®.
All rights reserved. Used with permission.

who show-ers us with bless-ing all our
who stands with those for - got-ten and con-
who calls us to be whole and to be

days.
fused.
free.

Born in Human Likeness 47

Born in hu-man like-ness, found in hu-man form: Je - sus, "God is

with us," we pro - claim your glo - ry!

A simple round based upon Philippians 2:7-11. The open harmony at the end is intentional, signifying unending praise – try leaving it unresolved.

Words and music: Bruce Harding. 2002
Words and music copyright © 2002 by Bruce Harding, www.evensong.ca. Used by permission.

48 I Can Feel You Near Me God
(Jump for Joy)

1 I can feel you near me God I can feel you near
2 I can feel you lov-ing me yes I know you care

Yes I know you're with me God I feel you here
God I know you're lov-ing me al - ways ev-ery-where

I can feel you near me God I can feel you near
I can feel you lov-ing me yes I know you care

Yes I know you're with me God Hea - ven is here.
God I know you're lov-ing me I know you're there.

And I'll jump for joy I'm sing-ing Al-le - lu-ia Jump for joy for

you I will jump for joy I'm sing-ing Al- le - lu-ia

Jump for joy for you.

Last time

Words and music: Pat Mayberry, 2000; arr. Margaret Stubbington, 2006
Words and music copyright © 2000 Pat Mayberry, SOCAN. www.patmayberry.com. Used by permission.
Arrangement copyright © 2006 Margaret Stubbington. Used by permission.

49 When We Seek Language

1 When we seek lan-guage to praise you, O God,
2 Stead-fast-ly lov-ing, you gave us your Word,
3 To be our guard-ian, sup-port-er, and guide,

all we can ut-ter seems stale, tame, or odd.
liv-ing a-mong us on earth, seen and heard,
you sent your Spir-it to stay by our side,

Tongue-tied and word-lost, we strug-gle to find
teach-er and heal-er whose prom-ise came true,
source of com-mu-ni-ty, well-spring of prayer,

phras-es that slight nei-ther heart, soul, nor mind:
dy-ing and ris-ing to make all things new:
pow-er to strength-en, and cour-age to dare:

Words: Carl P. Daw, Jr., 2005
Music: Carl F. Schalk, 2006
Words copyright © 2005 and music copyright © 2006 Hope Publishing Company.
Carol Stream, IL 60188. All rights reserved. Used by permission.

PERICHORESIS
10 10 10 10 with refrain

Alleluia (Duncan)   50

Try introducing this simple Alleluia one part at a time, from the top down.

Words: traditional liturgical text
Music: Norah Duncan IV
Music copyright © 1987 by GIA Publications, Inc. All rights reserved. 7404 S. Mason Ave., Chicago, IL 60638. www.giamusic.com. 800-442-1358.
Used by permission.

51 Yahweh Be Praised

Yah-weh be praised in the heav - ens.
Yah-weh be praised in the streets.
Yah - weh be praised with our sing - ing
when in wor - ship we meet. Yah-weh be
praised. Yah-weh be praised. Yah-weh be

Words and music: Paul Rumbolt; arr. Neil Weisensel, 2006
Words and music copyright © by Paul Rumbolt McCarthy. Please visit www.paulrumbolt.com for information. Used by permission.
Arrangement copyright © 2006 Neil Weisensel. SOCAN. www.neilmusic.com. Used by permission.

Alleluia (Uruguay)

52

A traditional song among the descendants of African slaves in Uruguay. Try it with guitar accompaniment and with maracas and other percussion.

Words: traditional liturgical text. Music: traditional melody, Uruguay. Arrangement: *More Voices*, 2007.
Arrangement copyright © .

53 God Who Spread the Boundless Prairie

♩ = 96

1 God who spread the bound-less prai-rie when the an-cient
2 God who came to us in Je-sus, loved us, suf-fered,
3 God who forms a di-verse peo-ple, call us to a
4 God who raised our roll-ing foot-hills crowned with moun-tain

o-ceans died; brought to birth the tribes and na-tions
died and rose; guide us well and give us wis-dom
com-mon task, grace and strength you free-ly give us
peaks be-yond; call us now to love and serve you,

born in dig-ni-ty and pride; now as one we
as the pace of know-ledge grows. Lord* re-mind us
when in prayer we hum-bly ask. Ra-ces, gen-ders,
joy-ful-ly will we re-spond. God whose glo-ry

seek your spir-it, reach-ing for your lov-ing hand, called by you our
when you call us to de-ci-sions, ways un-known, once for al-ways
you have made us dif-ferent, yet your great in-tent joins us in one
past and pres-ent lights us on our fu-ture way, now bap-tize us

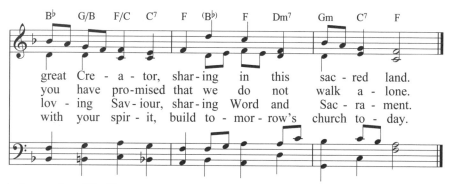

great Cre - a - tor, shar - ing in this sac - red land.
you have pro - mised that we do not walk a - lone.
lov - ing Sav - iour, shar - ing Word and Sac - ra - ment.
with your spir - it, build to - mor - row's church to - day.

* alternative: "God"

A prayer for unity and purpose.

Words: Herbert O'Driscoll, 2002
Music: Judith Snowdon, 2006
Words copyright © 2002 by Herbert O'Driscoll. Used by permission.
Music copyright © 2006 by Judith Snowdon. Used by permission.

Alleluia (Monteiro)   **54**

Al - le - lu - ia, al - le - lu - ia,

al - le - lu - ia.   ia.

Harmonize this Brazilian song freely, using the notes in the top stave. Repeat many times, beginning slowly then gradually increasing tempo and intensity before settling in to the close.

Words: traditional liturgical text
Music: Simei Monteiro
Music copyright © 1999 by Choristers Guild, Garland, TX 75041 All rights reserved. Used by permission.

55 Watch Once More the Windswept Storm Clouds
(Song of Waters)

Unison

1 Watch once more the wind-swept storm clouds;
2 Taste the mois-ture of the morn - ing,
3 View a - new the dark blue o - cean,
4 Feel the breath of God move soft - ly,

sud - den-ly the sky has wings! God has come to
smooth - er than the best red wine; toast the life - blood
whales ca-vort-ing, spray-ing foam; God at play with
gen - tle mists that brush the skin; Earth is breath - ing

rain a - mong us, giv - ing hope to all dry things.
of the plan - et: here's to God's wild wet de - sign!
deep sea mon-sters, feel - ing ver - y much at home.
God's own spir - it, life re-newed from deep with - in.

Harmony

Sing a song of splash - ing wa - ters,
Sing a song of flow - ing wa - ters,
Sing a song of laugh - ing wa - ters,
Sing a song of liv - ing wa - ters,

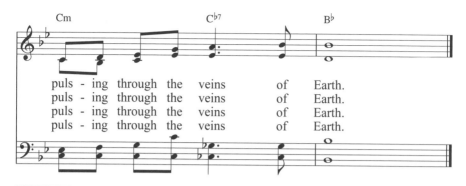

Cm	C♭7	B♭

puls - ing through the veins of Earth.
puls - ing through the veins of Earth.
puls - ing through the veins of Earth.
puls - ing through the veins of Earth.

Words: Norman Habel, 2000
Music: Neil Weisensel, 2006
Words copyright © 2000 Norman Habel. Administered by Willow Publishing Pty. Ltd.
All rights reserved. Used by permission.
Music copyright © 2006 Neil Weisensel. SOCAN. www.neilmusic.com. Used by permission.

NITA
878787
Alternate tune: LAUDA ANIMA
(PRAISE MY SOUL)

Come, O Come, Let Us Praise   56
(Lajahle, htaora Hp'ya)

♩ = 69

Burmese: 1 La - jah - le, hta - o - ra Hp'ya, hta - o - ra
(translit.) 2 La - jah - le, Kri - taw Hp'ya Kri - taw
3 La - jah - le, wing - iñ Hp'ya wing - iñ

English: 1 Come, O come, let us praise Par - ent
2 Come, O come, let us praise Jes - us
3 Come, O come, let us praise Spir - it

Hp'ya i mye - ta - daw ko - chi - moañ zoh - ley,
Hp'ya i Je - zu - daw ko - chi - moañ zoh - ley,
Hp'ya i mye - tha ha - yah ko - chi - moañ zoh - ley,

God, O praise the love of God, the great I Am,
Christ, O praise the grace of Christ, the Prince of Peace,
God, the fel - low - ship of Ho - ly Spir - it God,

mye - ta - daw ko - chi - moañ zoh - ley.
Je - zu - daw ko - chi - moañ zoh - ley.
mye - tha ha - yah ko - chi - moañ zoh - ley.

praise the love of God, the great I Am.
praise the grace of Christ, the Prince of Peace.
fel - low - ship of Ho - ly Spir - it God.

A song of praise to the Trinity, meant to be sung in unison, unaccompanied.

Words and music: Saw Gideon Tun Shwe, Myanmar, University Christian Fellowship, Myanmar
Words and music copyright © 1990, 2000 Christian Conference of Asia. Used by permission.

57 I'll Praise Eternal God
(Je louerai l'Éternel)

French: Je loue-rai l'É-ter-nel de tout mon cœur, je
English: I'll praise e-ter-nal God with all my heart, and

ra - con-te-rai tou-tes tes mer-veilles, je chan-te-rai ton
I will re-count your mar - vel-lous works and glo - ri-fy your

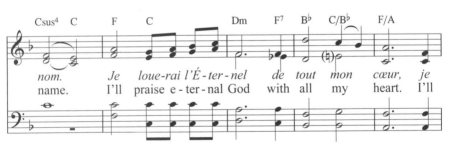

nom. Je loue-rai l'É-ter-nel de tout mon cœur, je
name. I'll praise e - ter-nal God with all my heart. I'll

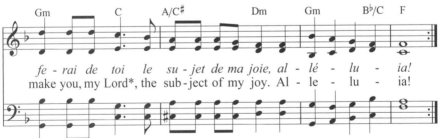

fe - rai de toi le su - jet de ma joie, al - lé - lu - ia!
make you, my Lord*, the sub-ject of my joy. Al - le - lu - ia!

* alternative: "my God"

Words (French) and music: Claude Fraysse; English translation and arrangement: John L. Bell, 2002
Words and music copyright © Claude Fraysse. Used by permission.
English translation and arrangement copyright © 2002 by WGRG, Iona Community, Scotland, admin. GIA Publications, Inc., excl. N. American agent.
All rights reserved. Used by permission.

We Sing of Your Glory

(Tuya es la gloria)

58

♩ = 88 E♭ — Fm — A♭7 — B♭ — B♭7 — E♭

Spanish: 1 Tu - ya es la glo - ria la hon - ra tam - bién;
2 Tu - yos los do - mi - nios, los tro - nos tam - bién;
3 A ti yo me rin - do, te a - do - ro tam - bién;

English: 1 We sing of your glo - ry, we praise you a - gain,
2 We sing of your pow - er and ho - nour a - gain,
3 We sing of sur - ren - der to you, God, a - gain.

Cm — Fm — A♭6 — B♭ — B♭7 — E♭

tu - ya pa - ra siem - pre. A - mén. A - mén.
tu - yos pa - ra siem - pre. A - mén. A - mén.
a - mor ab - so - lu - to. A - mén. A - mén.
for you are e - ter - nal. A - men. A - men.
for you are e - ter - nal. A - men. A - men.
Your power is e - ter - nal. A - men. A - men.

4. Glo-ria en las al-tu-ras
y en la tie-rra tam-bién;
glo-ria, al-le-lu-ya.
A-mén. A-mén.

4. "Glo-ry in the high-est,
on earth," sing a-gain.
Glo-ry, al-le-lu-ia. A-men. A-men.

French:

1. À toi soit la gloi-re,
À toi soit l'hon-neur,
À toi, pour les siè-cles;
A-men, a-men.

2. À toi, la puis-san-ce,
À toi, la gran-deur,
À toi, pour les siè-cles;
A-men, a-men

3. À toi, nous nous con-fions
Et nous t'a-do-rons,
A-mour im-mu-a-ble;
A-men, a-men.

4. Gloi-re sur la ter-re
Au plus haut des cieux.
Amen, al-lé-lu-ia,
A-men, a-men.

Words and music: traditional song, Latin America
English trans. S T Kimbrough, Jr.; French trans. David Fines, 2005; arr. *More Voices*, 2007
English translation copyright © 1996 General Board of Global Ministries, GBGMusik, 475 Riverside Dr., New York, NY 10115. All rights reserved.
Used by permission.
French translation copyright © 2005 David Fines. Used by permission.

59

Alleluia, Praise to God
(Aleluya Y'in Oluwa)

♩ = 100

Yoruba:
1. A - le - lu - ya Y'in O - lu - wa   A - le - lu - ya Y'in
2. E k'or - in   a - yo s'O - lu - wa   E k'or - in   a - yo
3. E k'or - in e lu' - lu f'O - lu - wa   E k'or - in e lu' - lu

English:
1. Al - le - lu - ia,   praise to God.   Al - le - lu - ia,
2. Songs of joy sing   out to God.   Songs of joy sing
3. Beat the drums, sing   out to God.   Beat the drums, sing

O - lu - wa   O seun, o seun, o seun,   o seun ba - ba
s'O - lu - wa   ka f'o - pe fun ka   si   tun ma - a jo
f'O - lu - wa   O seun, o seun, o seun,   o seun ba - ba

praise to   God.   Prais - es, high prais - es,   we bring you, O God.
out to   God.   Danc - ing and sing - ing,   we praise you, O God.
out to   God.   Prais - es, high prais - es,   we bring you, O God.

A - le - lu - ya Y'in O - lu - wa
e   k'or - in   a - yo s'O - lu - wa
e   k'or - in e   lu' - lu f'O - lu - wa

Al - le - lu - ia,   praise to   God.
Songs   of joy   sing   out to   God.
Beat   the drums,   sing   out to   God.

A Yoruba song of praise from Nigeria, **pronunciation:**

1. Ah-lay-loo-yah yihn oh-loo-wah... oh shyoon, oh shyoon, oh shyoon bah-bah...
2. Ay kohr-ihn ah-yoh soh-loo-wah... kah foh-pay foon kah see toon mah-ah joh...
3. Ay kohr-ihn ay loo-loo foh-loo-wah... oh shyoon, oh shyoon, oh shyoon bah-bah...

Words and music: traditional Yoruba song, Nigeria, as taught by Emmanuel Badejo.
English translation: Emmanuel Badejo, altered, *More Voices,* 2007.
Musical arrangement and English translation copyright © Emmanuel Badejo. Permission sought.

God, We Give You Heartfelt Praise 60
(Chú goán kámsia oló Lí)

Round
♩ = 92

Taiwanese: *Chú goán kám-sia o-ló Lí, Chú goán kám-sia*
English: God, we give you heart-felt praise, God, we give you

o - ló Lí, Lí un - tián thiàn - thàng
heart - felt praise, mer - cy and love you

lîn - bín bô - han, goán chôe - sian o - ló chheng - chàn.
show us dai - ly, bles - sed al - ways be your name.

A lively round from Taiwan, echoing the psalms.

Words: Timothy Tan
Music: Tai, Nai-Chen
Words and music copyright © 2000 Christian Conference of Asia. Used by permission.

I Praise You, O God 61

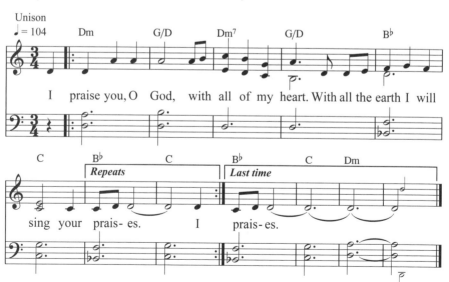

Unison
♩ = 104

Dm G/D Dm⁷ G/D B♭

I praise you, O God, with all of my heart. With all the earth I will

C B♭ C B♭ C Dm

Repeats sing your prais- es. *Last time* I prais- es.

A shorter song of praise suitable as an acclamation or a psalm refrain.

Words and music: David Robertson, after Psalm 138:1
Words and music copyright © 2005 by David Robertson, High River United Church, Box 5520, High River, AB Canada T1V 1M4. Used by permission.

62 There Is Room for All
(Chacun a sa place)

English: There is room for all in the sha-dow of God's wing;
French: Cha-cun a sa place á l'a-bri sous l'aile de Dieu;

there is room for all, shel-tered in God's love.
Cha-cun a sa place en l'a-mour de Dieu.

And I re-joice and sing, "My re - fuge and my
De joie, je chan-te-rai: "Mon re - fuge en le -

rock, in whom I trust." There is room for all,
quel je me con - fie." Cha-cun a sa place,

there is room for all!
cha-cun a sa place.

This song of the inclusive love of God echoes the opening verses of Psalm 91.

Words and music: Bruce Harding, 2004; French trans. David Fines, 2006
Words and music copyright © 2004 by Bruce Harding, www.evensong.ca. Used by permission.
French translation copyright © 2006 by David Fines. Used by permission.

Long before My Journey's Start

1 Long be-fore my jour-ney's start, when in my youth I
2 From the blos-som to the seed, long has she filled my
3 When I stretched my hands to the sky, when in des-pair my

searched in my heart, I would pray for her, wait for her,
cup in need, may I cling to her vine, taste of her wine,
soul raised a cry, I was saved by her gaze, led in her ways,

Wis - dom, my road, my goal, and my star.
Wis - dom, my life, my per - fect de - sign.
Wis - dom, my love, the light of my days.

Words: Steven C. Warner, based on Ecclesiasticus 51:13-22
Music: Leslie Palmer Barnhart
Words and music copyright © 1993, World Library Publications, 3708 River Rd., Suite 200, Franklin Park, IL 60131-2158. 800-566-6150. www.wlpmusic.com.
All rights reserved. Used by permission.

64 Because You Came

Words: Shirley Erena Murray, 1992.
Music: Amanda Husberg, 1996.

MAUJER STREET
9 8 10 9

Words and music © 1996 Hope Publishing Company, Carol Stream, IL 60188. All rights reserved. Used by permission.

When We Are Tested

1 When we are tes-ted and wres-tle a-lone,
2 When in the des-ert we cry for re-lief,
3 When we are temp-ted to bar-ter our souls,
4 When we have strug-gled and searched through the night,

fam-ished for bread when the world of-fers stone,
plead-ing for paths marked by cer-tain be-lief,
tra-ding the truth for the pow'r to con-trol,
sort-ing and sift-ing the wrong from the right,

nour-ish us, God, by your word and your way,
lift us to love you be-yond sign and test,
teach us to wor-ship and praise on-ly you,
Sav-iour, sur-round us with cir-cles of care,

food that sus-tains us by night and by day.
trust-ing your pre-sence, our on-ly true rest.
seek-ing your will in the work that we do.
an-gels of heal-ing, of hope, and of prayer.

A hymn rooted in the wilderness struggles of Jesus.

Words: Ruth Duck, 1996
Music: Ruth Watson Henderson, 2006
Words copyright © 1996 Hope Publishing Company, Carol Stream, IL 60188. All rights reserved. Used by permission.
Music copyright © 2006 Ruth Watson Henderson. Used by permission.

WHEN WE ARE TESTED
10 10 10 10
Alternate tune: SLANE

66 Senzeni Na?

A song from the struggle for freedom in South Africa.
Translation: *"What have we done?"* **Zulu pronunciation:** *Sehn-zeh-nee nah.*

Words and music: traditional song, South Africa; arr. *More Voices*, 2007
Arrangement copyright © .

Kyrie Eleison (Bridget)

This Kyrie works well with or without the choral accompaniment.

Words: traditional liturgical text; French trans. David Fines and David-Roger Gagnon, 2006
Music: John L. Bell
Music copyright © 1998 by WGRG, Iona Community, Scotland, admin. GIA Publications, Inc., excl. N. American agent.
All rights reserved. Used by permission.
French translation copyright © 2006 by David Fines and David-Roger Gagnon. Used by permission.

68 Kyrie Eleison (Guarani)

Try this traditional Kyrie in harmony, or sing it in unison with gentle "oo's," either improvised or as written in the top line. **Guarani pronunciation:** *oh-ray pohr-ya-whoo veh-reh-koh nyan-day-yah-rah.*

Words and music: traditional Guarani song, Paraguay, as taught by Pablo Sosa; French trans. David Fines, 2006
Descant: as taught by Pablo Sosa; arrangement: *More Voices*, 2005
French translation copyright © 2006 by David Fines. Used by permission.
Descant copyright © Pablo Sosa. Used by permission.
Arrangement copyright © 2007 The United Church of Canada.

Kyrie Eleison (Kervin) 69

Greek: Ky-ri-e e-le-i-son, ky-ri-e e-le-i-son, ky-ri-e e-le-i-son, ky-ri-e e-le-i-son.
French: Ô Sei-gneur, prends pi-tié, ô Sei-gneur, prends pi-tié, ô Sei-gneur, prends pi-tié, Sei-gneur, prends pi-tié de nous.

This Kyrie will sing well in unison or with the full SATB harmony.

Words: traditional liturgical text; French trans. David Fines, 2006 Music: William S. Kervin, 2005; arr. Bryn Nixon, 2006
French translation copyright © 2006 by David Fines. Used by permission.
Music copyright © 2005 William S. Kervin. Used by permission.
Arrangement copyright © 2006 Bryn Nixon. Used by permission.

Kyrie Eleison (Reindorf) 70

Greek: Ky-ri-e e-le-i-son. Ky-ri-e e-le-i-son. Ky-ri-e e-le-i-son.
English: Lord, have mer-cy on us. Lord, have mer-cy on us. Lord, have mer-cy on us.
French: Ô Sei-gneur, prends pi-tié de nous. Ô Sei-gneur, prends pi-tié de nous. Sei-gneur, prends pi-tié de nous.

A simple Kyrie from Ghana which works well unaccompanied or with improvised accompaniment.

Words: traditional liturgical text; French trans. David Fines, 2006 Music: Dinah Reindorf, 1987
French translation copyright © 2006 by David Fines. Used by permission.
Music copyright © 1987 Dinah Reindorf. Admin. Augsburg Fortress. Used by permission.

71 When the Wind of Winter Blows
(Warm the Time of Winter)

1 When the wind of win-ter blows, bring-ing times of sol - i - tude, fill the si - lent ic - y night; be our hearts' com - pas - sion.

2 When we shiv - er in des-pair, when the chill of death comes near, hold us, Spir - it, calm our fear, while the eve - ning deep - ens.

3 When in days of fall-en snow, change con-founds or love burns low, from the ash - es may there rise phoe-nix of our grow - ing.

Words: Ruth Duck, 1992
Music: Lori True, 2000
Words copyright © 1992 and music copyright © 2000 GIA Publications, Inc. All rights reserved. 7404 S. Mason Ave., Chicago, IL 60638. www.giamusic.com.
800-442-1358. Used by permission.

72 Why Stand So Far Away

1 Why stand so far a - way, my God? Why
2 Why do you hide when, full of lies, they
3 The weak are crushed and fall to earth; the
4 In a - ges past you heard the voice of
5 A - rise, O God, and lift your hand; bring

hide in times of need? The proud, un - bri - dled,
mur - der and be - tray? They wait to pounce up -
wick - ed strut and preen. Why in these cruel, cha -
those the proud op - press. Re - mem - ber those who
jus - tice to the poor. Come, help us stop the

chase the poor, and curse you in their greed.
on the weak as li-ons stalk their prey.
◆ ot - ic times can-not your face be seen?
suf - fer now, who cry in deep dis - tress.
flow of blood! Let ter - ror reign no more!

A hymn of lament and call for action based on Psalm 10.

Words: Ruth Duck, 1992
Music: Michael Mahler, 2003
Words copyright © 1992 and music copyright © 2003 GIA Publications, Inc.
All rights reserved. 7404 S. Mason Ave., Chicago, IL 60638. www.giamusic.com. 800-442-1358.
Used by permission.

WHY STAND SO FAR AWAY
8 6 8 6
Alternate tune: MORNING SONG

73 O God, Why Are You Silent?

1 O God, why are you silent? I
2 Now lost with-in my griev-ing, I
♦ 3 My hope lies bruised and bat-tered, my
4 Through end-less nights of weep-ing, through
5 May pain draw forth com-pas-sion, let

can-not hear your voice. The proud and strong and
fall and lose my way, my frag-ile, faint be-
♦ wound-ed heart is torn; my spir-it spent and
wea-ry days of grief, my heart is in your
wis-dom rise from loss. O take my heart and

vio-lent all claim you and re-joice. You
liev-ing so swift-ly swept a-way. O
♦ shat-tered by life's re-lent-less storm. Will
keep-ing, my com-fort, my re-lief. Come,
fash-ion the im-age of your cross. Then

Chords (line 1): Dm⁶ Em F Dm⁶ F/C C

prom - ised you would hold me with
God of pain and sor - row, my
◆ you not bend to hear me, my
share my tears and sad - ness, come,
may I know your heal - ing through

Chords (line 2): F C Dm A D⁷/F♯ G C/E G

ten - der - ness and care. Draw near, O Love, en -
com - pass and my guide, I can - not face the
◆ cries from deep with - in? Have you no word to
suf - fer in my pain; O bring me home to
heal - ing that I share, your grace and love re -

Chords (line 3): C⁶ D G C F/A C/G F⁶ G C

fold me, and ease the pain I bear.
mor - row with - out you by my side.
◆ cheer me when night is clos - ing in?
glad - ness, re - store my hope a - gain.
veal - ing your ten - der - ness and care.

Words: Marty Haugen
Music: Hans Leo Hassler, 1601; arr. Johann Sebastian Bach, 1729
Words copyright © 2003 by GIA Publications, Inc. All rights reserved. 7404 S. Mason Ave., Chicago, IL 60638. www.giamusic.com.
800-442-1358. Used by permission.

PASSION CHORALE
7 6 7 6 D

74 When Painful Mem'ries

1 When pain-ful mem'ries haunt each day and dreams dis-turb the
2 When dreams at last bring peace and rest, and fear has lost con-

night, when life is washed with shades of grey and
trol, when, tried by strug-gle, we are blessed with

phan-toms fill our sight, Christ, stay be-side us and em-brace the
right-ful mind and soul, stay close be-side us as be-fore, to

child who dwells with - in; come, Heal - er, touch our
guide us all our days. Christ, take the lives that

Words: Ruth Duck, 1994
Music: Sally Ann Morris, 1995
Words copyright © 1997 The Pilgrim Press. Used by permission.
Music copyright © 1998 GIA Publications, Inc. All rights reserved.
7404 S. Mason Ave., Chicago, IL 60638. www.giamusic.com. 800-442-1358. Used by permission.

MOSHER
8 6 8 6 D
Alternate tune: KINGSFOLD

lives with grace; re - store our lives a - gain.
you re-store and fit them for your praise.

Veni Sancte Spiritus   75
(Holy Spirit, come to us)

Latin: Ve - ni San-cte Spi - ri - tus, tu - i a-mo-ris i-gnem ac - cen-de.
English: Ho - ly Spir- it, come to us, kin-dle in us the fire of your love.

Ve - ni San-cte Spi - ri - tus, ve - ni San-cte Spi - ri - tus.
Ho - ly Spir- it, come to us. Ho - ly Spir- it, come to us.

Words: Taizé Community
Music: Jacques Berthier
Words and music copyright © 1998 Taizé Community, France, admin. GIA Publications, Inc., excl. N. American agent. All rights reserved.
Used by permission.

76 If I Have Been the Source of Pain
(Si fui motivo de dolor)

Unison
♩ = 80

Spanish:
1 Si fui mo - ti - vo de do - lor, oh Dios; si por mi
2 Si va-na y fú - til mi pa - la - bra fue; si al que su-
3 Si por la vi-da qui-se an-dar en paz, tran-qui - lo,

English:
1 If I have been the source of pain, O God; if to the
2 If I have spo-ken words of cru - el - ty; if I have
3 If I've in - sist-ed on a peace-ful life, far from the

cau-sa el dé - bil tro - pe - zó; si en tus ca -
fri - a en su do - lor de - jé; no me con -
li - bre y sin lu - char por ti cuan-do an-he -

weak I have re - fused my strength; if, in re -
left some suf-fering un - re - lieved; con - demn not
strug-gles that the gos - pel brings, when you pre -

mi - nos you no qui-se an-dar, ¡per - dón, oh Dios!
de - nes, tú, por mi mal-dad, ¡per - dón, oh Dios!
la - bas ver-me en la lid, ¡per - dón, oh Dios!

bel - lion, I have strayed a - way; for - give me, God.
my in - sen - si - tiv - i - ty; for - give me, God.
fer to guide me to the strife, for - give me, God.

(stanza 4) A - men, A - men.

A sung prayer of confession, the text for this song began as the gospel song, "If I have wounded any soul today." It was translated into Spanish before being retranslated into English again.

Words (Spanish): Sara M. de Hall, based on a text by C. M. Battersby; English trans. Janet W. May. 1992
Music: Pablo Sosa, 1988
English translation copyright © 1992 The Pilgrim Press. Used by permission.
Music copyright © 1988 Pablo Sosa, Argentina. Used by permission.

CAMACUA
10 10 10 4

4. Es-cu-cha oh Dios, mi hu-mil-de con-fe-sión
y lí-bra-me de ten-ta-ción su-til;
pre-ser-va siem-pre mi al-ma en tu re-dil.
A-mén, A-mén.

4. Re-ceive, O God, this ar-dent word of prayer,
and free me from temp-ta-tion's sub-tle snare,
with ten-der pa-tience, lead me to your care.
A-men, A-men.

Be Still and Know

77

A simple round in two parts with an optional choral/keyboard accompaniment.

Words: Psalm 46:1.
Music: John L. Bell.
Music copyright © 1989 & 1998 by WGRG, Iona Community, Scotland, admin. GIA Publications, Inc., excl. N. American agent. All rights reserved.
Used by permission.

78   # God Weeps

1 God weeps at love with-
2 God bleeds at an- ger's
3 God cries at hun- gry
4 God waits for stones to

held, at strength mis - used, at chil-dren's
fist, at trust be - trayed, at wo - men
mouths, at run - ning sores, at crea-tures
melt, for peace to seed, for hearts to

in - no-cence a-bused, and till we change the way we
bat-tered and a - fraid, and till we change the way we
dy - ing with-out cause, and till we change the way we
hold each oth - er's need, and till we un - der-stand the

love, God weeps.
win, God bleeds.
care, God cries.
Christ, God waits.

Words: Shirley Erena Murray, 1994
Music: Jim Strathdee, 1998

DELGADO
10 8 10
Words copyright © 1996 Hope Publishing Company, Carol Stream, IL 60188. All rights reserved. Used by permission.
Music copyright © 1998 Jim and Jean Strathdee (Desert Flower Music), PO Box 1476, Carmichael, CA 95609l (916) 481-2999.
www.strathdeemusic.com Used by permission.

Spirit, Open My Heart

Spir-it, o - pen my heart to the joy and pain of liv - ing.

As you love may I love, in re-ceiv - ing and in giv-ing,

Spir-it, o - pen my heart.

1 God, re - place my ston - y heart
2 Write your love u - pon my heart
3 May I weep with those who weep,

with a heart that's kind and ten - der. All my cold -
as my law, my goal, my sto - ry. In each thought,
share the joy of sis - ter, broth - er. In the wel -

ness and fear to your grace I now sur - ren-der.
word, and deed, may my liv - ing bring you glo - ry.
come of Christ, may we wel-come one an - oth - er.

Words: Ruth Duck, 1994
Music: traditional melody, Ireland; arr. Arthur G. Clyde, 1997
Words copyright © 1996 and arrangement copyright © 1997 The Pilgrim Press. Used by permission.

WILD MOUNTAIN THYME
7 8 6 8 with refrain

80   Beyond the Beauty and the Awe

Unison
♩ = 63

1 Be - yond the beau - ty and the awe,
2 Our lives feel torn be - tween the world
3 Oh, teach us how to hear your voice
4 In sound or si - lence, sight or smell,
5 Then help us live as Je - sus taught,

be - yond the fear and dread, we
whose needs are grim - ly real and
des - pite the traf - fic's din; to
may we some to - ken find that
as light and salt and yeast, that

long, O God, to hear your word,
emp - ty talk of peace and joy
keep the blasts of ran - cour out
makes your liv - ing pres - ence known
oth - ers may be brought to share

Words: Carl P. Daw, Jr., 1994
Music: Patrick Michaels, 1995
Words copyright © 1994 Hope Publishing Company, Carol Stream, IL 60188.
All rights reserved. Used by permission.
Music copyright © 1995 by Patrick Michaels. Used by permission.

ROFINOT
8 6 8 6
Alternate tune: MORNING SONG

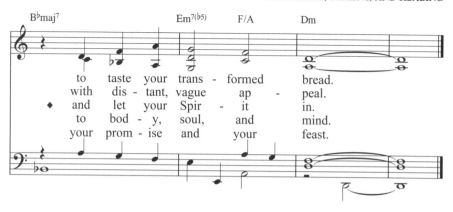

B♭maj7 Em7(♭5) F/A Dm

to taste your trans - formed bread.
with dis - tant, vague ap - peal.
and let your Spir - it in.
to bod - y, soul, and mind.
your prom - ise and your feast.

Love Us into Fullness 81

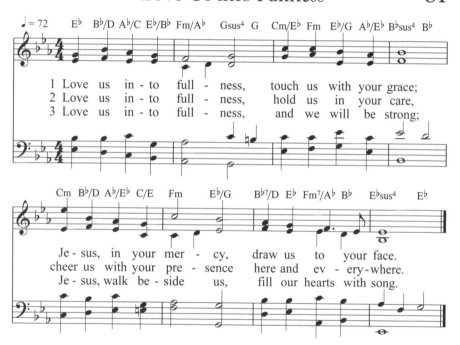

♩ = 72 E♭ B♭/D A♭/C E♭/B♭ Fm/A♭ Gsus4 G Cm/E♭ Fm E♭/G A♭/E♭ B♭sus4 B♭

1 Love us in - to full - ness, touch us with your grace;
2 Love us in - to full - ness, hold us in your care,
3 Love us in - to full - ness, and we will be strong;

Cm B♭/D A♭/E♭ C/E Fm E♭/G B♭7/D E♭ Fm7/A♭ B♭ E♭sus4 E♭

Je - sus, in your mer - cy, draw us to your face.
cheer us with your pre - sence here and ev - ery-where.
Je - sus, walk be - side us, fill our hearts with song.

Words and music: Daniel Charles Damon, 2002
Words and music copyright © 2006 Hope Publishing Company, Carol Stream, IL 60188.
All rights reserved. Used by permission.

BURLINGAME
6 5 6 5
Alternate tunes: ERNSTEIN or
BEMERTON (CASWALL)

82

Bathe Me in Your Light

1 Bathe me in your light, O God of All, Cre - a - tor;
2 Bathe me in your love, O Source of Awe and Won - der;
3 Bathe me in your grace, O One of Spir - it's long - ing;

let it shine u - pon my soul with heal - ing and with grace.
help me walk the sa - cred path of har - mo - ny and peace.
teach me of your gen - tle ways that fill the soul with strength.

Be to me a bea - con bright through sha - dows of life's wound - ing,
May I be at - ten - tive to the mus - ings of your pre - sence,
Guide me on the pil - grim - age that leads to truth and whole - ness,

show - ing me the way to live in faith, in your em - brace.
drink - ing from the well of hope that brings the heart re - lease.
Fill me with your pro - mise of a love that knows no length.

Words: John Oldham, 2002
Music: Ron Klusmeier, 2002
Words copyright © 2002 by John Wesley Oldham. Used by permission.
Music copyright © 2002 by Ron Klusmeier, www.musiklus.com. Used by permission.

Let My Spirit Always Sing

83

1 Let my spir - it al - ways sing, though my heart be
2 Though my bod - y be con - fined, let your word en -
3 Let your wis - dom grace my years, choose my words and
4 Let my spir - it al - ways sing, to your Spir - it

win - ter - ing, though the sea - son of de - spair
gage my mind, let the in - ner eye dis - cern
chase my fears, give me wit to wel - come change,
an - swer - ing, through the si - lence, through the pain

give no sign that you are there, God to whom my
how much more there is to learn, see the world be -
to ac - cept, and not es - trange, let my joy be
know my hope is not in vain, like a feath - er

days be - long, let there al - ways be a song.
com - ing whole through the win - dow of the soul.
full and deep in the know - ledge that I keep.
on your breath trust your love, through life and death.

Words: Shirley Erena Murray
Music: Jane Marshall
Words copyright © 1996 Hope Publishing Company, Carol Stream, IL 60188. All rights reserved. Used by permission.
Music copyright © 2005 Jane Marshall. Used by permission.

SPIRITSONG
7 7 7 D
Alternate tune: INWARD LIGHT

84 In You There Is a Refuge

1 In you there is a re-fuge, in you we find our peace.
2 In you there is a vi-sion, in you we learn to dream.

When all we know is cha-os may our trust in you in-crease. In
When all we see is de-sert may you be our liv-ing stream. In

you there is a si-lence, in you our minds are clear. When
you there is a fu-ture, in you we find our way. When

all we hear is dis-cord may your qui-et draw us
hope has shed its bright-ness may you

near. show us a new day.

Word: Keri K. Wehlander, 2005
Music: Linnea Good, 2005
Words copyright © 2005 Keri K. Wehlander. www.creativeworship.ca. Used by permission.
Music copyright © 2005 Borealis Music. www.LinneaGood.com. Used by permission.

Take, O Take Me as I Am 85
(Oh! Prends-moi tel que je suis)

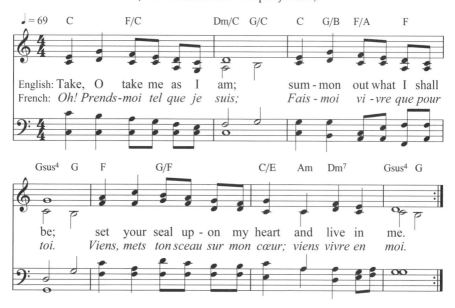

English: Take, O take me as I am; sum-mon out what I shall
French: *Oh! Prends-moi tel que je suis; Fais-moi vi-vre que pour*

be; set your seal up-on my heart and live in me.
toi. Viens, mets ton sceau sur mon cœur; viens vivre en moi.

This song of discernment intentionally ends on an open harmony. Try leaving it unresolved.

Words: John L. Bell and Graham Maule, 1995; French trans. David Fines, 2005
Music: John L. Bell, 1995
Words and music copyright © 1995 by WGRG, Iona Community, Scotland, admin. GIA Publications, Inc., excl. N. American agent. All rights reserved. Used by permission.
French translation copyright © 2005 by David Fines. Used by permission.

Da Pacem Cordium 86
(Give peace to ev'ry heart)

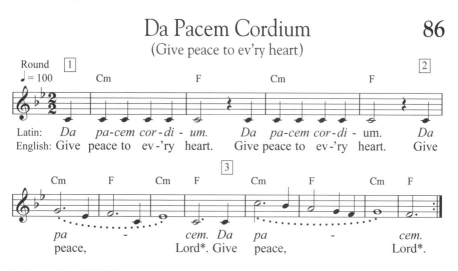

Latin: *Da pa-cem cor-di-um. Da pa-cem cor-di-um. Da*
English: Give peace to ev-'ry heart. Give peace to ev-'ry heart. Give

pa - cem. Da pa - cem.
peace, Lord*. Give peace, Lord*.

* alternative: "God"

A centring song, a prayer for peace and healing.

Words: traditional liturgical text. Music: Jacques Berthier.
Words and music copyright © 1991 Taizé Community, France, admin. GIA Publications, Inc., excl. N. American agent. All rights reserved. Used by permission.

87 Water Flowing from the Mountains
(Living Water)

Unison
♩ = 108

1 Wa - ter flow - ing from the moun - tains.
2 Wa - ter rush - ing down the ri - vers.
3 Wa - ter spring-ing from the dry place.

Wa-ter flow - ing o'er the earth.
Wa-ter rush - ing to the sea.
Wa-ter spring-ing in the sun.

Wa-ter comes to us, so
Wa-ter comes to us, so
Wa-ter comes to us, so

pre - cious. Liv-ing wa-ter gives us birth.
pre - cious. Liv-ing wa-ter makes us free.
pre - cious. Liv-ing wa-ter for each one.

Words and music: jim hannah, 2003; arr. David Melhorn-Boe, 2006
Words and music copyright © 2003 jim hannah. Used by permission.
Arrangement copyright © 2006 David Melhorn-Boe, 238 First Ave. E., North Bay, ON P1B 1J8. email: mboe@onlink.net.

ASSURANCE

88 Over My Head
(Aud'suss de moi)

♩ = 50 - 72

English: O - ver my head, I hear mu - sic in the air. O - ver my
French: Au - d'ssus de moi, c'est d'la mu - sique que j'en - tends. Au - d'ssus de

head, I hear mu - sic in the air. O - ver my head, I hear
moi, c'est d'la mu - sique que j'en - tends. Au - d'ssus de moi, c'est d'la

mu - sic in the air. There must be a God some - where. *Fine*
mu - sique que j'en - tends. Il y a un Dieu quel - que part.

Leader

1 When the storms of life are rag - in'
1 Quand tous les ou - ra - gans sé - vissent,

Ooh, I hear
Ooh, c'est d'la

This arrangement of a traditional African-American song is intended to be sung slowly and freely.

Words and music: African-American spiritual; French trans. Denise Souldore, 2006
Arrangement: Stephen Lee, 2006
French translation copyright © 2006 Denise Souldore. Used by permission.
Arrangement copyright © 2006 Professional Music Services. Used by permission.

Additional verses (English):

2. When the winds of strife are blowin'...
3. When the tide of hate is risin'...
4. King* Jesus is a-callin'...

Additional verses (French):

2. Quand les vents de la lut-te soufflent...
3. Quand la ma-rée de hai-ne monte...
4. C'est Jé-sus qui tous nous ap-pelle...

* alternative: "O"

89

Love Is the Touch

Unison
♩ = 144

1 Love is the touch of in - tan - gi - ble joy;
2 Love is the lilt in a lin - ger - ing voice;
3 Love is the light in the tun - nel of pain;
4 Love is the Ma - ker and Spir - it and Son;

love is the force that no fear can des - troy;
love is the hope that can make us re - joice;
love is the will to be whole once a - gain;
love is the king - dom their will has be - gun;

love is the good - ness we glad - ly ap - plaud:
love is the cure for the fright - ened and flawed:
love is the trust of a friend on the road:
love is the path which the saints all have trod:

God is where love is, for love is of God.
God is where love is, for love is of God.
God is where love is, for love is of God.
God is where love is, for love is of God.

A hymn about love, quoting 1 John 4:7, for weddings or general use.

Words: Alison M. Robertson, 1998
Music: John L. Bell, 1998
Words copyright © 1998 Alison M. Robertson, 3 Ross Gardens, Edinburgh, EH9 3BS, Scotland.
Music copyright © 1998 WGRG, GIA Publications, Inc. All rights reserved. 7404 S. Mason Ave.,
Chicago, IL 60638. www.giamusic.com . 800-442-1358. Used by permission.

AMOR DEI
10 10 10 10
Alternate tunes: OLDHAM or SLANE

Don't Be Afraid

(N'ayez pas peur)

♩ = 60

English: Don't be a-fraid. My love is strong-er, my love is strong-er than your fear.
French: N'a-yez pas peur, mon a-mour est plus fort, il est plus fort que vo - tre peur.

Don't be a-fraid. My love is strong-er and I have prom-ised, prom-ised to be al - ways near.
N'a-yez pas peur, mon a-mour est plus fort; je vous ai pro - mis, pro - mis d'ê-tre tou - jours là.

Words: John L. Bell and Graham Maule, 1995
French trans. David Fines, 2005
Music: John L. Bell, 1995
Words and music copyright © 1995, 2007 by WGRG, Iona Community, Scotland, admin. GIA Publications, Inc., excl. N. American agent.
All rights reserved. Used by permission.
French translation copyright © 2005 by David Fines. Used by permission.

91 Cradle Me in Your Arms
(Berce-moi en tes bras)

Cra-dle me in your arms, cher-ish and com-fort me. O Je-sus, source of heal - ing love, in your pres-ence I am free.

free.

French:

Ber-ce-moi en tes bras,
cal-me-moi, dor-lo-te-moi.
Jé-sus, tu es sour-ce d'a-mour,
je me sens libre a-vec toi.

Words and music: Bruce Harding, 2000; French paraphrase: David-Roger Gagnon and David Fines, 2006.
Words and music copyright © 2000 by Bruce Harding, www.evensong.ca. Used by permission.
French paraphrase copyright © 2006 by David-Roger Gagnon and David Fines. Used by permission.

Like a Rock

Actions for "Like a Rock":

Like a rock: Extend both forearms upward, palms facing down in one movement.

Like the starry night sky: Wiggle fingers while slowly raising arms to head height.

Like the sun: Extend one forearm, palm up. With palm down, slowly extend the other hand 6" over the first arm, arcing up at the end, so the palm is facing away from the body.

Like the river: Leave the first forearm as before. Other hand makes a "swimming" motion close to it, by weaving it gently in handshake position.

Evermore: End with "God's hug" – crossing arms over chest, hands to shoulders.

Words: Keri K. Wehlander, 1998
Adapted to music: Linnea Good, 1999
Words and music copyright © 1999 Borealis Music. www.LinneaGood.com. Used by permission.

93 What Calls Me from the Death

♩ = 126

1 What calls me from the death where I have rest - ed?
2 Now I can hear the voice of Je - sus call - ing,
3 The rem - nants of my past I now am shed - ding;
4 No mat - ter that my tomb was of long stand - ing,

Why am I now e - mer - ging from my tomb? I
but it is not the Sa - viour's voice a - lone, for
the bits of cloth that cling I now dis - card. And
that change seemed fu - tile, out of reach for me. If

sense that I am com - ing to be test - ed.
o - thers share their words as tears are fall - ing.
in this new di - rec - tion I am head - ing,
I ac - cept the life that God is hand - ing,

Is this my se - cond birth - ing from the womb?
Col - lec - tive - ly, they roll a - way the stone.
I know that I will find my own re - ward.
my bless - ing is a new i - den - ti - ty.

A hymn of resurrection, echoing the story of Lazarus, John 11:1-44.

Words: Mary R. Bittner, 2004 Music: Fred Kimball Graham, 2006
Words copyright © 2004 by Wayne Leupold Editions, Inc. Used by permission.
Music copyright © 2006 Emmanuel College, Toronto.
(Emmanuel College, 75 Queen's Park Cres, Toronto, ON M5S 1K7). ec@utoronto.ca. Used by permission.

NEW IDENTITY
11 10 11 10
Alternate tune: DEER PARK

Love Knocks and Waits

1 Love knocks and waits for us to hear, to
2 Love of-fers life, in spite of foes who
3 Love comes to heal the bro-ken heart, to
4 Love knocks and en - ters at the sound of

o - pen and in - vite; Love longs to qui - et
threat-en and con - demn; em - brac-ing en - e -
ease the troub - led mind; with - out a word Love
wel come from with - in; Love sings and danc - es

ev - ery fear, and seeks to set things right.
mies, Love goes the sec - ond mile with them.
bids us start to ask and seek and find.
all a - round, and feels new life be - gin.

Words and music: Daniel Charles Damon, 1994
Words copyright © 1996 and music copyright © 1998 Hope Publishing Company, Carol Stream, IL 60188.
All rights reserved. Used by permission.

ANGEL'S CAMP
8 6 8 6
Alternate tune: MORNING SONG

95 How Deep the Peace

♩ = 104

How deep the peace, the con-fi-dence, of those whose wrongs are for-
Deep peace, con-fi-dence, all for -

giv - en. How deep the peace, the con - fi -
giv'n. Deep peace, con - fi -

dence, of those whose hearts are healed.
dence, all are healed.

Words: Lynn Bauman, 2000
Music: Linnea Good, 2004
Words copyright © 2000 Lynn Bauman, from *Ancient Songs Sung Anew: the Psalms as Poetry*. Used by permission.
Music copyright © 2004 Borealis Music, www.LinneaGood.com. Used by permission.

96 And When You Call for Me

(Et lorsque tu m'appelles)

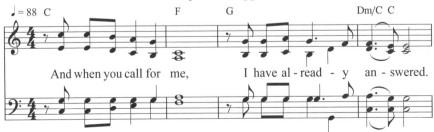

♩ = 88

And when you call for me, I have al - read - y an - swered.

And when you call for me, I am al-read-y there.

French:

Et lors-que tu m'ap-pelles,
que dé-jà j'ai ré-pon-du.

Et lors-que tu m'ap-pelles,
que dé-jà je suis là.

Words: Lynn Bauman, 2000; French trans. David Fines, 2006
Music: Linnea Good, 2004
Words copyright © 2000 Lynn Bauman, from *Ancient Songs Sung Anew: the Psalms as Poetry*. Used by permission.
Music copyright © 2004 Borealis Music, www.LinneaGood.com. Used by permission.
French translation copyright © 2006 by David Fines. Used by permission.

Listen, God Is Calling

97

(Lis-ten) Lis-ten, God is cal-ling, through the Word in-vi-ting,

of-fer-ing for-give-ness, com — fort and joy. (Lis-ten)

The harmonies for this assurance of forgiveness are only a suggestion, so feel free to make up your own.

Words and music: traditional song, Tanzania; trans. Howard S. Olson
Arrangement: *More Voices*, 2007
Translation copyright © Makumira University College (formerly Lutheran Theological College Makumira), PO Box 55, Usa River, Tanzania. Used by permission.
Arrangement copyright © 2007 The United Church of Canada.

98 Like a River of Tears
(Renewing Our Spirits)

1 Like a riv-er of tears your love pours up-on
2 Like a bird in free flight by win-dows a-round
3 Like a pil-lar of cloud you prom-ise to guide
4 Like a lov-er's ca-ress your spir-it re-vives

us; like a sun-shine of bless - ing your grace will sus-
us; like a wind in the for - est that breathes life a-
us; like a bright fi-ery bush you come to speak
us; like a song of the soul you come to be

tain us; like a star-stud-ded sky
mong us; like a phoe-nix that's ris -
to us; like a calm cool-ing breeze
with us; like a prayer of the heart

Words: John Oldham, 1996
Music: Ron Klusmeier, 1997
Words copyright © 1996 by John Wesley Oldham. Used by permission.
Music copyright © 1997 by Ron Klusmeier, www.musiklus.com. Used by permission.

99 Stand, O Stand Firm

Stand, O stand firm. Stand, O stand firm. Stand, O

Sis - ters*, stand ver - y stand firm and see what our God can do.

* make up additional verses: "Brothers," "People," "Children," etc.

The harmonies for this song of solidarity are only a guideline – feel free to make up your own.

Words and music: traditional song, Cameroon; arr. *More Voices*, 2007
Arrangement copyright © 2007 The United Church of Canada.

100 Lord God, You Love Us
(Toi, tu nous aimes)

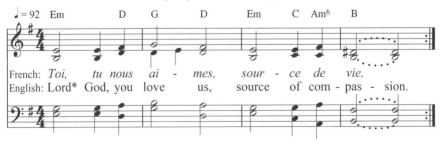

French: *Toi, tu nous ai - mes, sour - ce de vie.*
English: Lord* God, you love us, source of com - pas - sion.

* alternative: "O God"

Words: Taizé Community
Music: Jacques Berthier
Words and music copyright © Ateliers et Presses de Taizé (France). All rights reserved. Published and printed through exclusive license agreement by GIA Publications, Inc., 7404 S. Mason Ave., Chicago, IL 60638. www.giamusic.com. 800-442-1358. Used by permission.

Jesus, You Fill Our Hearts

101

Je - sus, you fill our hearts with your love, our
minds with your peace, and our lives with your joy.

Words and music: Daniel Charles Damon, 1998
Words and music copyright © 2006 Hope Publishing Company, Carol Stream, IL 60188. All rights reserved. Used by permission.

Jesus, Your Spirit in Us

102

English: Je - sus, your Spir - it in us is a well-spring of life ev - er - last - ing.
German: *Chri-stus, dein Geist wohnt in uns, er ist Quel - le des e - wi-gen Le- bens.*

Words and music: Taizé Community
Words and music copyright © 2005 Ateliers et Presses de Taizé (France). All rights reserved. Published and printed through exclusive license agreement by GIA Publications, Inc., 7404 S. Mason Ave., Chicago, IL 60638. www.giamusic.com. 800-442-1358. Used by permission.

103 Ka mana'o 'I 'O

The opening phrase of this Hawaiian song translates as "Faithful is our God."
Hawaiian pronunciation: *Kah-mah-nah-oh ee oh, oh koh kah-koo ah-koo-ah.*

Words and music: Joe Camacho, 1999
Words and music copyright © 1999 by Joe Camacho. Used by permission.

dark - ness. / love. / way, / kind - ness.
The God who shares the breath of / For God is good, and / to be God's hands and heart with / And in our jour - ney, may

life with you and me, / holds us as we sleep, / ten - der-ness and care. / love lead the way.
all liv - ing things up - on the earth. / to wake us to the morn-ing light. / God's faith - ful - ness is al - ways there. / To be God's liv - ing, sing this day.

Know That God Is Good 104
(Mungu ni mwema)

Swahili: Mu- ngu ni mwe-ma, mu-ngu ni mwe-ma,
English: Know that God is good, know that God is good,
French: C'est vrai: Dieu est bon! C'est vrai: Dieu est bon!
Luganda: Ka-ton-da mu-lun-gi, ka - ton-da mu-lun- gi,

mu - ngu ni mwe-ma, ni mwe - ma, ni mwe- ma.
know that God is good, God is good, God is good.
C'est vrai: Dieu est bon! Dieu est bon! Dieu est bon!
ka - ton-da mu-lun- gi, mu-lun- gi, mu-lun- gi.

Swahili pronunciation: Moo-ngoo nee mway-mah.
Luganda pronunciation: Kah-ton-dah moo-loon-jee.

Words and music: traditional song, Congo; arr. Edo Bumba; French trans. David Fines, 2005.
French translation copyright © 2005 David Fines. Used by permission.
Arrangement copyright © Edo Bumba. Used by permission.

105

You Are My Father

(Too'n mera pita)

sab - uh - nee   tha - yee'n.
in all plac - es, ev - ery - where.

Taa'n bhayo ke - haa
How can I feel sor - row?

kaa - ra jee - yo.
How can I e - ver be a - fraid?

D.C. al Fine

kaa - ra jee - yo.
How can I e - ver be a - fraid? O,

This song which echoes the Hebrew psalms is drawn from the Sikh scriptures, and is part of a much longer kirtan or devotional hymn. The opening section can be sung on its own, without the solo verse. The rhythm is Deepchandi Taal, a fourteen-beat pattern which subdivides into 3+4+3+4.

Punjabi pronunciation, with the following principles in mind:
- *the "'n" sound in "too'n," "thayee'n" and "taa'n" should be a nasalized "n" sound*
- *"t" at the beginning of a word is a "t" sound, while "t" in the middle of a word should be a cross between a "t" and a "d" sound*
- *the initial vowel in "bandhup" should be very brief, so you sing on the "n" sound*

Too'n meh-rah pih-tah, too'n heh meh-rah mah-tah,
too'n meh-rah buhnn-duhp ah, too'n meh-rah brah-tah.
Too'n meh-rah rah-kah sahb-uh-nee tah-yee'n.
Tah'n byoh keh-hah kah-rah jee-yoh.

Words: traditional Sikh liturgical text; English trans. Harkanwal Singh Sahota, 2006
Music: Harkanwal Singh Sahota and Amarjeet Singh Vabhana, 2006
English translation copyright © 2006 by Harkanwal Singh Sahota. Used by permission.
Music copyright © 2006 by Harkanwal Singh Sahota and Amarjeet Singh Vabhana. Used by permission.

106 I Am the Dream

1 I am the dream and you the dream-er.
2 I am the bell and you the sil-ence.
3 You are the word and I the e-cho.

I am the song and you are the rhyme.
You are the yearn-ing I can-not cur-tail.
You are the lead-er and I am the led.

You are the tune sung in ev-'ry si-lence.
I am the blest and you the bles-sing.
You are the joy and I the laugh-ter.

You are the now in the end-less stream of time.
You are the wilds in which I lose my trail.
You are the Rock on which I lay my head.

A hymn based on images drawn from Rainer Maria Rilke's The Book of Hours.

Words: S. Curtis Tufts, 2005
Music: Rick Gunn, 2006
Words copyright © S. Curtis Tufts 2005 – 178 Greenwood Drive, Spruce Grove, AB T7X 1Y7. Used by permission.
Music copyright © 2006 Rick Gunn. www.rickgunn.com. Used by permission.

AVERY
irregular
Alternate tune: GODPOINT

God Loves Me

(Elolo nye Mawu elolo nguto)

Ewe: E - lo - lo, nye Ma - wu e - lo - lo ngu - to, e -
English: God loves me, for my God is love, di - vine love. God

ke - ke, mi - doe de dzi. E - lo - lo, nye Ma - wu e -
pro - tects me: God is great. God loves me, for my God is

lo - lo ngu - to, e - ke - ke, mi - doe de dzi.
love, di - vine love. God pro - tects me: God is great.

Ewe pronunciation: *Ay-lah-lah, nyay Mah-oo ay-lah-lah ngoo-toh, ay-kay-kay, mee-doh day dsee*

Words and music: traditional song, Togo and Ghana
English para: S.T. Kimbrough, 2004.   Arrangement: *More Voices*, 2007
English paraphrase copyright © 2004 General Board of Global Ministries, GBG Musik, 475 Riverside Dr., New York, NY 10115. All rights reserved.
Used by permission. Arrangement copyright © .

108 I Know Your Word
(Tua Palavra)

Portuguese: Tu-a Pa-la-vra é lâm-pa-da pa-ra os meus pés, Se-nhor. Tu-a Pa-la-vra é lâm-pa-da pa-ra os meus pés Se-nhor. Lâm-pa-da pa-ra os meus

Spanish: Es tu Pa-la-bra lám-pa-ra pa-ra mis pies, Se-ñor. Es tu Pa-la-bra lám-pa-ra pa-ra mis pies, Se-ñor. Lám-pa-ra pa-ra mis

English: I know your Word, your Word is a lamp to my feet, O God. I know your Word, your Word is a lamp to my feet, O God. I know your Word is a

A lively prayer for illumination.

Words: Psalm 119:105, adapted by Simei Monteiro; English trans. Simei Monteiro and Joan Sutton; French trans. David-Roger Gagnon, 2006
Music: Simei Monteiro
Words, music and translation copyright © 2000 General Board of Global Ministries, GBGMusik, 475 Riverside Dr., New York, NY 10115.
All rights reserved. Used by permission.
French translation copyright © 1996 David-Roger Gagnon. All rights reserved. Used with permission.

French:

Oui Ta Pa-role est une Lu-mière pour mes pas, Ô Dieu (2x)

Oui elle est u-ne Lu-mière, Ô Dieu, u-ne Lu-mière pour mes pas. (2x)

109 My Soul Is Thirsting for You

♩ = 112

My soul is thirst-ing for you, O Lord*, thirst - ing for you, my God.

My soul is thirst - ing for you, O Lord*, thirst-

ing for you, my God, thirst - ing for you, my God.

Repeat chorus | *To verses* | *Last time* | Fine

Turn page for verse 3

* alternative: "O God"

Try this song as a congregational refrain with solo or choral verses.

Words (refrain): The International Commission on English in the Liturgy (ICEL)
Words (verses) and music: Steve Angrisano, 1997
Music and verse text copyright © 1997 Steve Angrisano. Published by spiritandsong.com ®. All rights reserved. Used with permission.
Refrain text copyright © ICEL. All rights reserved.

3 I will nev - er be a - fraid, for I will not be a - ban-

doned. E - ven when the road grows long and wea - ry your

love will res - cue me.

First-born of Mary

First-born of Ma - ry, pro - voc - a - tive prea - cher, it -
in - er - ant tea - cher, out - sid - er's choice; Je - sus in - spires
and dis - arms and con - fus - es who -
ev - er he choos - es to hear his voice.

Words and music: John L. Bell, 1998
Words and music copyright © 1998 by WGRG, Iona Community, Scotland, admin. GIA Publications, Inc., excl. N. American agent.
All rights reserved. Used by permission.

111 A Voice Was Heard in Ramah

1 A voice was heard in Ra - mah that could not be con-soled, as
2 O God, we hear the cry - ing for lit - tle ones of yours; for
3 When - e - ver one is weep - ing, the whole world suf-fers, too. Yet,
4 O Prince of Peace, you lead us in ways of truth and grace. May

Ra-chel wept for chil - dren she could no long-er hold. For
ma - ny still are dy - ing in con-flicts and in wars in
Je - sus, as we serve them, we're al - so ser-ving you. So
we be brave to prac - tice your peace in ev - ery place to

He - rod ruled the na - tion, yet feared the In - fant King. How
ev - ery trou - bled na - tion, on ev - ery vio - lent street, how
may we not ig - nore them, nor turn our eyes a - way, but
love each fear - filled na - tion, to serve each troub-led street, how

great the de - va - sta - tion that fear and an - ger bring!
great the la - men - ta - tion when fear and an - ger meet!
help us la - bour for them to bring a bet - ter day.
great the cel - e - bra - tion when peace and jus - tice meet!

A hymn for peace based on the story of the Slaughter of the Innocents in Matthew 2.

Words: Carolyn Winfrey Gillette, 2004
Music: Welsh folk melody; Evan's *Hymnau a Thonau*, 1865; arr. *English Hymnal*, 1906
Words copyright © 2004 by Carolyn Winfrey Gillette.

LLANGLOFFAN
7 6 7 6 D
Alternate tune: PASSION CHORALE

Amen, Amen, It Shall Be So

♩ = 66

1 Blest are the poor in spir - it, the
2 Blest are the sor-row - ful, the sor-row - ful, they
3 Blest are the gen - tle, the gen - tle, the
4 Blest are the hun - gry for jus - tice, they
5 Blest are the mer -ci - ful, the mer -ci - ful, they
6 Blest are the pure in heart, for

Words sung as antiphon, notes hummed as verse accompaniment

Am   Dm⁷   G   Cmaj⁷

A - men, a-men, it shall be so! A -

king - dom of heaven is theirs.
shall be com - fort - ed.
earth shall be their own.
shall be sa - tis - fied.
shall find mer - cy shown.
they shall see their God.

F   Bm⁷⁽♭⁵⁾   E

men, al - le - lu - ia!

Additional solo verses:

7. Blest are the earth's peace-ma-kers, each
   one shall be God's child.

8. Blest are those vic-tim-ized for do-ing
   good, the king-dom of heaven is theirs.

This congregational refrain works well on its own or with the solo verses from the Beatitudes sung above.

Words and music: John L. Bell, 1997, after Matthew 5:3-10
Words and music copyright © 1997 by WGRG, Iona Community, Scotland, admin. GIA Publications, Inc., excl. N. American agent. All rights reserved. Used by permission.

113 Jesus Saw Them Fishing
(Fish with Me)

1 Je - sus saw them fish-ing by the shore of Gal - i-lee,

2 rich young per-son came to Je - sus look-ing for ad-vice.

3 "If you want to fol-low me, de - ny your ver-y self.

cast-ing out their nets in - to the sea.

"How can I ob-tain e - ter-nal life?"

Take up your cross and walk the walk with me.

Try this song as a congregational refrain with solo or choral verses.

Words and music: Ken Canedo, 2002
Words and music copyright © 2002, Ken Canedo. Published by spiritandsong.com ®. All rights reserved. Used with permission.

Si-mon Pe-ter, An - drew and the sons of Zeb-e-dee,

Je-sus told him, "Hon-our the com-mand-ments of the Lord*.

This might seem a hard-ship, an im-pos-si-bil-i-ty,

wait-ing in their boats so pa-tient-ly.

Then sell off all your rich-es for the poor."

but noth-ing is im-pos-si-ble with God."

*alternative: "God"

Behold the Face of Christ

Be-hold the face of Christ. O Je - sus Christ, O

Liv - ing Christ, you rise a - mong your peo - ple.

Accompaniment (instrumental or choral) while scripture verses are read.

Scripture verses for reading:

1. But when, Lord?
   When did we see you hungry and give
      you food to eat?
   When did we see you, Lord?

2. But when, Lord?
   When did we see you thirsty and
      give you water to drink?
   When did we see you, Lord?

3. But when, Lord?
   When did we see a stranger and
      welcome you in?
   When did we see you, Lord?

4. But when, Lord?
   When did we see you naked and
      give you clothes to wear?
   When did we see you, Lord?

5. But when, Lord?
   When did we see you ill and
      come to sit at your bedside?
   When did we see you, Lord?

6. But when, Lord?
   When did we see you in prison and
      come to visit you?
   When did we see you, Lord?

7. But when, Lord?
   When did we see you – the Christ, the
      son of Mary, our brother, our God?
   When did we see you, Lord?

A gentle chant, interspersed with readings over keyboard or choral accompaniment.

Words and music: Bernadette Farrell, 2002
Words and music copyright © 2002 by Bernadette Farrell. Published by OCP Publications. All rights reserved. Used with permission..

115 Behold, Behold, I Make All Things New

Be-hold, (be-hold,) be-hold, (be-hold,) I make all things new, be-
gin-ning with you and start-ing from to-day. Be-
hold, (be-hold,) be-hold, (be-hold,) I make all things new, my
pro-mise is true, for I am Christ the way.

A simple refrain for women and men's voices in two parts, with an optional alto pedal line.

Words and music: John L. Bell, 1995
Words and music copyright © 1995 by WGRG, Iona Community, Scotland, admin. GIA Publications, Inc., excl. N. American agent.
All rights reserved. Used by permission.

The Thirsty Deer

(Comme un cerf soupire après l'eau)

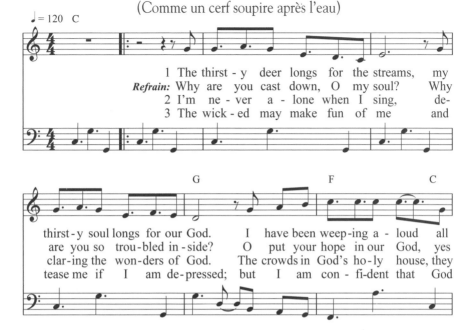

1 The thirst-y deer longs for the streams, my
Refrain: Why are you cast down, O my soul? Why
2 I'm ne-ver a-lone when I sing, de-
3 The wick-ed may make fun of me and

thirst-y soul longs for our God. I have been weep-ing a-loud all
are you so trou-bled in-side? O put your hope in our God, yes
clar-ing the won-ders of God. The crowds in God's ho-ly house, they
tease me if I am de-pressed; but I am con-fi-dent that God

day and all night, as I long for the face of our God.
God is our help, O sing prais-es to our liv-ing God.
all join with me just to pro-claim how God's great and good.
will res-cue me, yes, God's al-ways done this in times past.

French:

1. Comme un cerf sou-pire a-près l'eau
de même je sou-pire a-près toi.
Mes lar-mes sont le pain de mes jours et
mes nuits
car j'ai soif de ta pré-sence, ô Dieu.

Refrain
Pour-quoi es-tu si a-bat-tue?
Et gé-mis-tu en moi, mon âme?
Mets ton es-poir en Dieu qui est no-tre
ro-cher
chan-te les lou-anges en son hon-neur.

2. Je n'suis pas seul lors-que je chante
a-vec le cor-tège, je m'a-vance
vers le tem-ple du Sei-gneur a-vec
la joie et
a-vec des cris de re-con-nais-sance.

3. Mes en-ne-mis m'in-sul-tent sans cesse.
Me faut-il vivre dans la tris-tesse?
J'ai con-fi-ance que Dieu mon-tre-ra
son a-mour
car Il est en-core Sau-veur et Dieu.

A lively Calypso song.

Words: Psalm 42, paraphrased (English and French) by George Mulrain
Music: traditional melody, Caribbean; arr. Godfrey Taylor
Words and music copyright © 1996 General Board of Global Ministries, GBGMusik, 475 Riverside Dr., New York, NY 10115.
All rights reserved. Used by permission.

117 By the Well, a Thirsty Woman

Unison
♩ = 80

1 By the well, a thirs-ty wo-man found the life that you could
2 Plant us firm, like trees by wa-ter, send our roots down deep in
3 May we be your streams of jus-tice, as the wa - ter, may we

give, we, too, thirst like emp - ty ves - sels –
you, quench our parched and thir - sty spir - its
move through your peo - ple – by your Spir - it

fill us full that we may live. Je - sus,
with your wa - ter, pure and true. Je - sus,
show-ing mer - cy, shar - ing love. Je - sus,

source of liv-ing wa - ter, Well-spring bub-bling deep with - in,
source of liv-ing wa - ter, Nour - ish - er of all on earth,
source of liv-ing wa - ter, Ground-swell forc - ing truth to view,

Words: Elizabeth Stilborn, 1998, rev. 2005
Music: Diana Wilcox, 2006
Words copyright © 2005 by Beth Stilborn. Used by permission.
Music copyright © 2006 Diana Wilcox, Thunder Bay, ON. Used by permission.

RESPLENDENT
8 7 8 7 D
Alternate tune: EBENEZER

By the wa-ters of our bap - tism wis-dom pur-pose
By the wa-ters of our bap - tism quick-en growth and
By the wa-ters of our bap - tism set us free to

life be - gin.
give new birth.
live for you.

Me Alone 118

Me a - lone, me a - lone in-a the wil-der - ness.

For-ty days and for-ty nights in-a the wil-der - ness.

A simple call and response song rooted in the desert experience of Jesus.

Words and music: traditional song, Jamaica; arr. Patrick Prescod
Arrangement copyright © The Caribbean Conference of Churches. Used by permission.

119 God Our Protector

God our pro - tec - tor, keep us in mind,

al - ways give strength to your peo - ple. For if

we could be with you one day in time it is

bet - ter than a thou - sand with - out you.

A shorter song based on Psalm 84:8-10. The song works well with or without the instrumental bridge.

Words and music: Steve Bell, 1989
Words and music copyright © 1993 Signpost Music, www.signpostmusic.com. Used by permission.

120 My Soul Cries Out
(Canticle of the Turning)

A paraphrase of the Magnificat, Luke 1:46-55.

Words: Rory Cooney, 1990
Music: traditional melody, Ireland; arr. Rory Cooney, 1990
Words and arrangement copyright © 1990 by GIA Publications, Inc. All rights reserved.
7404 S. Mason Ave., Chicago, IL 60638. www.giamusic.com. 800-442-1358. Used by permission.

STAR OF THE COUNTY DOWN (KINGSFOLD)
Irregular

burn. Wipe a - way all tears, for the

jus - tice burn.

dawn draws near, and the world is a-bout to turn!

world is a - bout to turn!

121 Hey Now! Singing Hallelujah!

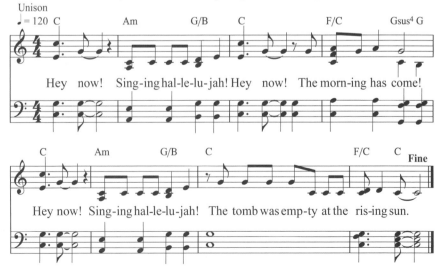

Hey now! Sing-ing hal-le-lu-jah! Hey now! The morn-ing has come!

Hey now! Sing-ing hal-le-lu-jah! The tomb was emp-ty at the ris-ing sun.

Words and music: Linnea Good, 1998
Words and music copyright © 1998 Borealis Music. www.LinneaGood.com. Used by permission.

122

This Is the Day
(Voici le jour)

English: This is the day that God has made; we will re-joice and be glad!
French: *Voi-ci le jour que Dieu a fait; nous le vi-vrons dans la joie.*

This is the day that God has made; we will re-joice and be glad!
Voi-ci le jour que Dieu a fait; nous le vi-vrons dans la joie.

Sing-ing hal-le-lu, sing-ing hal-le-lu,
Chan-tant Al-le-lu! Chan-tant Al-le-lu!

(oh, sing-ing)
(Oh, chan-tant)

sing-ing hal-le-lu! We will re-joice and be glad!
Chan-tant Al-le-lu! Nous le vi-vrons dans la joie.

Words and music: Bruce Harding, 2003, after Psalm 118:24
French trans. David Fines, 2005
Words and music copyright © 2003 by Bruce Harding, www.evensong.ca. Used by permission.
French translation copyright © 2005 by David Fines. Used by permission.

Sing-ing hal-le- lu, sing-ing hal-le- lu, sing-ing
Chan-tant Al-le- lu! Chan-tant Al-le- lu! Chan-tant

(oh, sing-ing)
(Oh, chan-tant)

hal - le - lu! We will re - joice and be glad!
Al - le - lu! Nous le vi - vrons dans la joie.

Day after Day 123

Day af - ter day, night af - ter night,

you speak through ev - ery - thing. thing.

A psalm refrain or prayer response based on Psalm 16:7

Words: Lynn Bauman, 2000
Music: Linnea Good, 2005
Words copyright © 2000 Lynn Bauman, from *Ancient Songs Sung Anew: the Psalms as Poetry.* Used by permission.
Music copyright © 2005 Borealis Music, www.LinneaGood.com. Used by permission.

124 Glory to God in the Highest

♩ = 132

Glo - ry to God in the high - est and peace to God's peo - ple on earth.

Glo - ry to God in the high - est and peace to God's peo - ple on earth

Repeats ... *Last time* earth.

Make up vocal harmonies for this lively Caribbean Gloria.

Words: traditional liturgical text
Music: Trinidad workshop, Caribbean Conference of Churches; arr. Patrick Prescod
Music and arrangement copyright © The Caribbean Conference of Churches. Used by permission.

When a Grain of Wheat
(Hitotsubu no)

Unison
♩ = 72

Japanese:
(translit.) *Hi - to - tsu - bu no   mu - gi wa o - chi - ke - ri*
English: When a   grain of wheat,   in - to the ground   has fall - en,

chi - no   u - e ni   ma - ta ha - e -   i - zu - ru
in - to the cold ground,   and lies in wait - ing for the spring,

ha - ru o   ma -   chi - tsu - tsu   ma - ta ha - e -
and lies in   wait -   ing for the spring;   this fall - en   grain

i - zu - ru,   ha - ru o   ma -   chi - tsu - tsu.
will rise to life,   this fall - en   grain   will rise to life!

A resurrection hymn by one of Japan's most esteemed Christian activists and poets.
Japanese pronunciation: *Hee-toh-tsoo-boo noh moo-gee wah oh-chee-keh-ree chee-noh oo-ay nee mah-tah hah-ay-ee-zoo-roo hah-roo oh mah-chee-tsoo-tsoo. (The "r" sound in Japanese should be a flipped "r", similar to a quick "l" sound).*

Words: Toyohiko Kagawa; English trans. Frank Y. Ohtomo
Music: Ushio Takahashi
Words copyright © 1981 Sumimoto Kagawa, Kagawa Foundation. Used by permission.
Music: copyright © Ushio Takahashi. Used by permission.
English translation copyright © Estate of Frank Y. Ohtomo. Used by permission.

126   Are You a Shepherd?

Unison
♪ = 144

1 Are you a shep - herd, good shep - herd who leads us
2 Are you a moth - er, good moth - er who bears us,
3 Great, gen - tle shep - herd, for - ev - er be - side us,

safe - ly through dan - ger, while calm - ing our fears?
com - forts, pro - tects us and helps us to rest?
lead all your chil - dren in paths that are right.

Are you a fa - ther who shel - ters and feeds us,
Are you a teach - er who dai - ly pre - pares us,
Great, lov - ing par - ent, wise teach - er, you guide us.

shares in our laugh - ter and wipes a - way tears?
chal - leng - ing stu - dents to of - fer their best?
We want to love you and bring you de - light.

Refrain

Yes, you are shep-herd, par-ent and teach-er, but you are great-er than all that we know. Ho - ly and liv-ing, lov - ing and giv-ing, God, you are with us wher - ev - er we go.

Words: Ruth Duck, 2002
Music: William P. Rowan, 2002
Words and music © 2002 Selah Publishing Co., Inc., www.selahpub.com. All rights reserved. Used by permission.

ZILKER PARK
11 10 11 10 with refrain

127

I Saw the Rich Ones
(Work for a World)

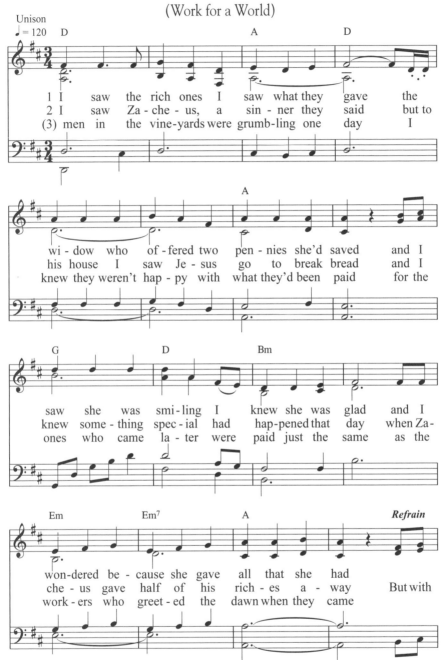

Unison
♩ = 120

1 I saw the rich ones I saw what they gave the
2 I saw Za-che-us, a sin-ner they said but to
(3) men in the vine-yards were grumb-ling one day I

wi-dow who of-fered two pen-nies she'd saved and I
his house I saw Je-sus go to break bread and I
knew they weren't hap-py with what they'd been paid for the

saw she was smi-ling I knew she was glad and I
knew some-thing spec-ial had hap-pened that day when Za-
ones who came la-ter were paid just the same as the

won-dered be-cause she gave all that she had
che-us gave half of his rich-es a-way But with
work-ers who greet-ed the dawn when they came

God the world is turned up - side down the poor are em -
braced and the lost they are found Let's work for a world where all
peo - ple are free where it's good to feel good a - bout God
lov - ing you and me. 3 The me.

Words and music: Pat Mayberry, 2000; arr. Margaret Stubbington, 2006
Words and music copyright © 2000 Pat Mayberry, SOCAN. www.patmayberry.com. Used by permission.
Arrangement copyright © 2006 Margaret Stubbington. Used by permission.

128 When They Heard That Jesus Was Coming

One

𝅘𝅥 = 108

1 When they heard that Je - sus was com - ing,
2 Spread their cloaks and branch - es be - fore him,
3 Blest is he, like Da - vid be - fore him.
4 Guid - ing cloud and pil - lar of fire,
5 Word of God, and first - born of peo - ple,
6 Vi - sion blest, and hope for the fu - ture,

All

Sing ho - san - na to the cho - sen one!

One

All the peo - ple went out to meet him.
Chil - dren sang with palm branch - es wav - ing.
Blest is he, God's bless - ing up - on him.
Sa - tan's foe and friend of the sin - ner.
Prom - ise kept, the crown of cre - a - tion.
God's be - lov - ed, ra - diant with glo - ry.

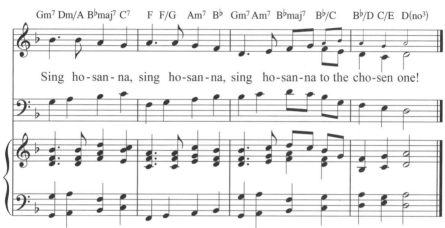

7. Won-drous bread, and stream in the des-ert, ...
   Ho-ly thirst, and God's liv-ing wa-ter. ...

8. Eye of God, who see to the heart of us, ...
   Heal-ing touch, the sight of our blind-ness. ...

9. Ris-ing sun, the light of the world, ...
   Word of life, who give us your Spir-it. ...

10. Friend in death, who weep for our dy-ing, ...
    Friend in death, who roll back the stone for us. ...

11. Friend in death, who wake us to new life, ...
    Friend in life, we sing glad ho-san-nas. ...

A song echoing the language of early antiphons, for Palm Sunday and throughout the year.

Words and music: Rory Cooney, 1999
Words and music copyright © 1999 GIA Publications, Inc. All rights reserved. 7404 S. Mason Ave., Chicago, IL 60638.
www.giamusic.com. 800-442-1358. Used by permission.

129 To the High and Kindly Hills

Nae-ga san-ŭl hyang-ha-yŏ nun-ŭl dŭ-ne
To the high and kind-ly hills I lift my eyes;

na-ŭi do-um-i ŏ-di-sŏ o-nŭn-ga
where is some-one to res-cue me in my plight?

na-ŭi do-um-i ch'ŏn-ji-rŭl   ji ŭ - shin.
Tru-ly from the dear Lord* a-bove help will come.

Yŏ - ho-wa ha-na-nim - e - ge-sŏ   o - ne.
God is the Mak-er of heaven and earth: all is well.

* **alternative:** "Truly from our God"

Korean pronunciation:
Nay-ga san-uhl hyang-ha-yoh noo-nuhl deu-nay
na-yay doh-uh-mee uh-dee-soh oh-neun-ga
na-yay doh-uh-mee chun-jee-ruhl Jee-eu-shihn.
Yoh-hoh-wa Ha-na-nihm ay-gay-soh oh-nay.

The accompanying taegum (bamboo flute) and kayagum (plucked zither) parts can be played on instruments such as flute and pizzicato cello, or they can be played together as treble and bass staves on piano or organ. Chang-go is a double-headed drum which is played on both heads, one for low sounds and the other for high. Substituting with any combination of low and high drum sounds will work fine.

Words: Im, Song-suk, Korea, after Psalm 121:1-2
Music: Lee, Song-chon, Korea
Words and music copyright © Christian Conference of Asia. Used by permission.

130 Rise Up, Rise Up

soul.   Rise up and sing this bles - sing to God's name.

Words and music: Linnea Good, 2003
Words and music copyright © 2004 Borealis Music, www.LinneaGood.com. Used by permission.

131 You, Creator God, Have Searched Me

Unison
♩ = 144

1 You, Cre-a-tor God, have searched me   and you know my ways.
2 You cre-a-ted light and dark-ness   and you love them both.

You per - fect-ly un-der-stand me. It's my cause of praise.
You blessed the womb of my moth-er, you brought me to birth.

I can-not es-cape your pres-ence in air, land or sea.
In your im-age and your like-ness won-der-ful-ly made.

Your arms of love and pro-tec-tion are al-ways with
I will lift my voice to praise you, you are God in-

me.
deed.

Chorus

You know me, O God, you have made me.

I am proud I'm the work of your hand.

In my wak-ing and sleep - ing mo - ments, with my

be - ing I will praise your name.

A lively calypso song.

Words and music: George Mulrain, paraphrasing Psalm 139; arr. *More Voices*, 2007

Words and music copyright © George Mulrain, Ordained Minister of the Methodist Church in the Caribbean and The Americas (MCCA). Used by permission. Arrangement copyright © .

132 Great Sorrow Prodded Jairus

Unison
♩ = 84

1 Great sor-row prod-ded Jair-us to seek the Heal-er's
2 Through years of pain and tor-ment the wo-man yearned for
3 Wher-ev-er peo-ple hun-ger for faith and hope and

touch— "My lit-tle girl is dy-ing, I
peace, while peo-ple scorned and shunned her, she
trust, where peo-ple search for whole-ness, for

need your help so much." When Je-sus stood be-
prayed her pain would cease. When Je-sus felt her
treat-ment that is just— Christ, give your heal-ing

side her, he took the child's limp hand, he
pre-sence, he touched her tremb-ling hand, "your
pre-sence, your strong and gen-tle hand, your

A hymn of healing based on Matthew 9:18-26.

Words: Elizabeth Stilborn, 2000
Music: Diana Wilcox, 2006
Words copyright © 2000 by Beth Stilborn. Used by permission.
Music copyright © 2006 Diana Wilcox, Thunder Bay, ON. Used by permission.

PIPER DOON
7 6 7 6 D
Alternate tune: PASSION CHORALE

Am   F   Dm   F/G   G   C

brought back life and laugh - ter by say - ing, "child, now stand."
ac - tions, daugh-ter, healed you, in faith and whole-ness, stand."
voice to lift us up - wards, by say - ing, "child, now stand."

Jesus Laughed Out Loud   133

Unison
♩ = 84   E♭   B♭/D   Cm   Cm/B♭   A♭   E♭

1 Je - sus laughed out loud to see the chil - dren
2 Je - sus healed a child by ask - ing her to
♦ 3 Je - sus felt the need; we made the crowd sit
4 Je - sus climbed a hill to pray and rest a -
5 Je - sus called my name when he was pass - ing

B♭sus⁴   B♭   B♭/D   E♭   B♭/D

play;   his joy - ful pres - ence
rise,   and doubt - ful peo - ple
♦ down.   A boy had faith and
lone;   we won - dered why we
by;   my life will nev - er

Cm   E♭/B♭   A♭   E♭   Fm   B♭⁷   E♭

drew a crowd we could not send a - way.
wept and smiled to see her o - pen eyes.
♦ all were fed, though we were far from town.
felt the chill of wind and wood and stone.
be the same; this love will nev - er die.

Words and music: Daniel Charles Damon, 1994
Words and music copyright © 2002 ABINGDON PRESS (Administered by THE COPYRIGHT COMPANY, NASHVILLE, TN).
All rights reserved. International Copyright Secured. Used by permission.

VOISIN
5 6 8 6

134 There Was a Child in Galilee

(Dreaming Mary)

Unison
♩ = 80

1 There was a child in Ga-li-lee who wan-dered wild a-long the
2 One ho-ly day an an-gel came with voice of wind and eyes of
3 And did she dream a-bout a son? And did he speak, the an-gel
4 Then Je-sus grew in Ga-li-lee, they wan-dered wild a-long the

sea. A ho-ly child, a-lone was she, and they
flame. He pro-mised blessed would be her name when he
one? We on-ly know God's will was done in the
sea. Now he calls to you and me to

called her Dream - ing Ma - ry. And she
spoke to Dream - ing Ma - ry. Then she
son of Dream - ing Ma - ry. Then she
dream with Dream - ing Ma - ry. And we

Chorus

dreamed, re-joic-ing in her sav - iour; she
spoke, re-joic-ing in her sav - iour. She
prayed, re-joic-ing in her sav - iour. She
dream, re-joic-ing in our sav - iour. We

F   Dm   C   B♭   Gm

dreamed of jus-tice for the poor.   She dreamed that kings op-pressed no
spoke of jus-tice for the poor.   She spoke that kings op-pressed no
taught him jus-tice for the poor.   She taught that kings op-pressed no
dream of jus-tice for the poor.   We dream that kings op - press no

Csus⁴ C   B♭   Csus⁴   C

more   when she dreamed, that Dream-ing Ma-ry.
more   when she spoke,   that Dream-ing Ma-ry.
more   when she taught,   that Dream-ing Ma-ry.
more   as we dream   with Dream-ing Ma-ry.

A song of the loves and dreams of Mary, rooted in the Magnificat, Luke 1:46-55.

Words and music: Janet Gadeski, 2005; arr. Patricia Wright, 2006
Words and music copyright © Janet Gadeski, The United Church of Canada Foundation, #300 – 3250 Bloor St. W., Toronto, ON M8X 2Y4. Used by permission.
Arrangement copyright © 2006 by Patricia Wright. Used by permission.

135 Called by Earth and Sky

(Du ciel et de la terre)

Called by earth and sky, prom-ise of hope held high. This is our sa - cred liv - ing trust, trea-sure of life sanc - ti - fied, called by earth and sky.

To verses

Last time
called by earth and sky, called by earth and sky.

A call to live with respect in Creation, celebrating the ancient tradition of the four elements.

Words and music: Pat Mayberry, 2005; French translation: David Fines, 2006
Arr. Margaret Stubbington, 2005

Words and music copyright © 2005 Pat Mayberry. www.patmayberry.com. Used by permission.
French translation copyright © 2006 by David Fines. Used by permission.
Arrangement copyright © 2005 by Margaret Stubbington. Used by permission.

1 Pre-cious these wa - ters, end - less seas,
2 Pre-cious this gift, the air we breathe;
3 Pre-cious these moun - tains, anc - ient sands;
4 Pre-cious the fire that lights our way,

deep o - cean's dream, wa - ters of heal - ing,
wind born and free. Breath of the Spir - it,
vast fra - gile land. Seeds of our wak - ening,
bright dawn - ing day. Fire of pas - sion,

riv - ers of rain, the wash of love a - gain.
blow through this place, our gath - ering and our grace.
root - ed and strong, Cre - a - tion's faith-ful song.
sor - rows un - done, our faith and jus - tice one.

French:

Refrain
Du ciel et de la terre,
nous en-ten-dons l'ap-pel;
nous de-vons ché-rir l'univers.
é-crin de vie, pré-cieuse et belle;
du ciel et de la terre.

1. Pré-cieu-ses sont les eaux
   im-menses des o-cé-ans,
   sour-ce de vie et de re-nais-sances,
   de l'a-mour le plus grand.

2. Pré-cieux est l'air que l'on res-pire,
   libre est le vent;
   Es-prit qui souf-fle, viens nous in-struire,
   de grâ-ce nous com-blant.

3. Pré-cieu-ses nous sont les mon-tagnes
   qui, de tous temps,
   gran-dio-ses ro-chers, nous
       ac-com- pagnent,
   de leur force et leur chant.

4. Pré-cieux le feu qui nous é-claire,
   les nuits, les jours,
   en nos pas-sions, nos cris, nos pri-ères,
   de jus-tice et d'a-mour.

136 When Hands Reach Out and Fingers Trace

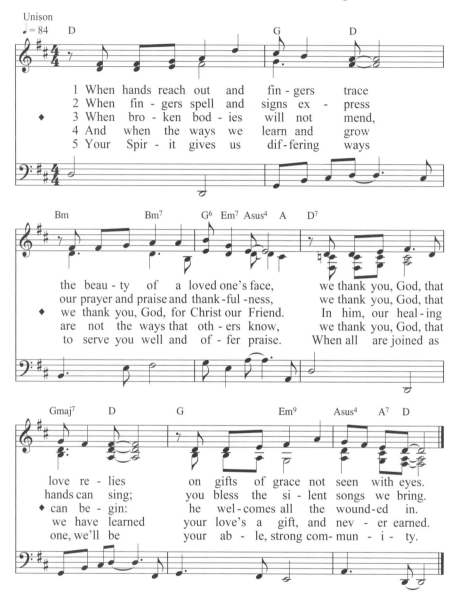

Unison
♩ = 84

1 When hands reach out and fin-gers trace
2 When fin-gers spell and signs ex-press
3 When bro-ken bod-ies will not mend,
4 And when the ways we learn and grow
5 Your Spir-it gives us dif-fering ways

the beau-ty of a loved one's face,
our prayer and praise and thank-ful-ness,
we thank you, God, for Christ our Friend.
are not the ways that oth-ers know,
to serve you well and of-fer praise.

we thank you, God, that
we thank you, God, that
In him, our heal-ing
we thank you, God, that
When all are joined as

love re-lies on gifts of grace not seen with eyes.
hands can sing; you bless the si-lent songs we bring.
can be-gin: he wel-comes all the wound-ed in.
we have learned your love's a gift, and nev-er earned.
one, we'll be your ab-le, strong com-mun-i-ty.

A hymn that celebrates differences in appearance and ability.

Words: Carolyn Winfrey Gillette, 2001
Music: Blair Odney, 2006; arr. Bruce Harding, 2006

SHILOH
8 8 8 8
Words copyright © 2001 by Carolyn Winfrey Gillette. All rights reserved. Used by permission.
Music copyright © 2006 by Blair Odney. Used by permission.
Arrangement copyright © .
Alternate tune: O WALY WALY or
TALLIS' CANON

Welcome, Jesus, You Are Welcome 137

1 Wel - come, Je - sus, you are wel-come in this world made hard by fear; lov - ing reach us, liv - ing teach us, Je - sus, you are wel - come here.

2 Wel - come, Je - sus, you are wel-come in the ghet - tos we have made; give the tat - tered, bruised and bat-tered win - ter shel - ter, sum - mer shade.

3 Wel - come, Je - sus, you are wel-come with the wealth - y and the poor; give the bro - ken love un - spo - ken, o - pen wide each pris - on door.

4 Wel - come, Je - sus, you are wel-come; let your lov - ing light ap - pear. In our see - ing, in our be - ing, Je - sus, you are wel - come here.

Words and music: Daniel Charles Damon, 1992, rev. 2004

SWEETWATER
8 7 8 7

Alternate tune: OMNI DIE (DIC MARIA)

Words and music copyright © 2006 Hope Publishing Company, Carol Stream, IL 60188.
All rights reserved. Used by permission.

138 My Love Colours Outside the Lines

(Outside the Lines)

Unison **Swing** ♩ = 132

1 My love col-ours out-side the lines,
2 My Lord col-ours out-side the lines,
3, 4 My soul longs to col-our out-side the lines,

ex - plor - ing paths that few could ev - er find;
turns wounds to bless - ings, wa - ter in - to wine;
tear back the cur - tains, sun, come in and shine;

and takes me in - to pla-
and takes me in - to pla-
I want to walk be - yond the boun-

ces where I've nev - er been be - fore, and o - pens
ces where I've nev - er been be - fore, and o - pens
daries where I've nev - er been be - fore, throw o - pen

Words and music: Gordon Light, 1995; arr. Andrew Donaldson
Words and music copyright © 1995 Common Cup Company, www.commoncup.com. Used by permission.
Arrangement copyright © Andrew Donaldson. Used by permission.

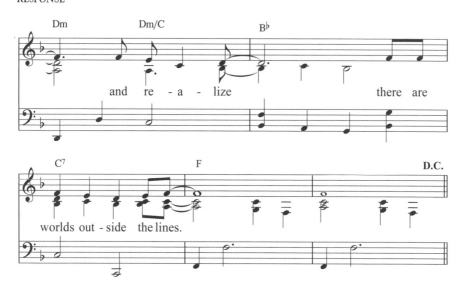

and re - a - lize there are

worlds out - side the lines.

139   True Faith Needs No Defence

1 True faith needs no de - fence, it ech - oes in the soul; a
2 True faith, like mu - sic, soars be - yond cath - e - dral walls; on
3 Ex - pect your faith to grow; be - gin by be - ing still, and
4 To live the faith we find, is all that love can ask; to

faith - ful life gives ev - i - dence of grace that makes us whole.
cit - y streets and o - cean shores, from age to age faith calls.
in the qui - et come to know God's liv - ing, breath-ing will.
sing God's praise with heart and mind, and rise to meet the task.

Words: Daniel Charles Damon, 1994, rev. 2004
Music: Daniel Charles Damon, 2004
Words and music copyright © 2006 Hope Publishing Company, Carol Stream, IL 60188.
All rights reserved. Used by permission.

ROCKLIN
6 6 8 6
Alternate tunes: GOLDEN HILL
or SOUTHWELL

As Long As We Follow

(Na nzela na lola)

Lingala: 1 Na nze-la na lo - la to-ko-tam-bo-la ma-lem - be, ma-
2 Na nze-la na lo - la to-ko-yem-ba na e - se-ngo ma-
3 Na nze-la na lo - la to-ko - te-ya na e - se-ngo ma-
4 Na nze-la na lo - la to-ko-bon-de-la ma-si-ya ma-

English: 1 As long as we fol - low in the way that God is lead-ing, we
2 As long as we hope*there is a fu-ture for cre - a - tion, a

Refrain (All)

lem - be to-ko-tam-bo-la.
lem - be to-ko-tam-bo-la.
lem - be to-ko-tam-bo-la. Ma-lem - be, ma-
lem - be to-ko-tam-bo-la.

know God's reign will sure-ly come.
fu - ture for the u - ni-verse. We know this, we

lem - be, ma-lem - be to-ko-tam-bo-la.
know this. Yes, God's reign will sure-ly come.

* additional verses: "pray" (or "sing") and "act"

Lingala pronunciation:
1. Nah zay-lah nah loh-lah toh-koh-tahm-boh-lah mah-lehm-bay...
2. Nah zay-lah nah loh-lah toh-koh-yehm-bah nah eh-sehn-goh...
3. Nah zay-lah nah loh-lah toh-koh-teh-yah nah eh-sehn-goh...
4. Nah zah-lah nah loh-lah toh-koh-bohn-deh-la ah-see-yah...

Words and music: Joseph Kabemba, Congo
Words and music copyright © 2004 General Board of Global Ministries, GBGMusik, 475 Riverside Dr., New York, NY 10115.
All rights reserved. Used by permission.

141

We Are All One People

(All One People)

♩ = 100 *All*

1, 2 We are all one peo-ple, we all come from one Cre-a-

Frame drum

tion way on high. We are all one

na-tion un-der one great sky, you and I.

We are all one peo-ple, we are all one

One

col-our {in her / in his} eyes. Weh yah

heh yah, weh yah heh yah, heh yah. Weh yah

This song by Saskatchewan Cree composers will work fine with only the English verses, leaving out the high middle section. However, the tradition of singing praise using vocables (syllables with no specific meaning meant to be vehicles for untexted praise) can be a spirit-filled experience for your community. Try the middle section, inviting the congregation and choir to sing freely, switching octaves as needed to sing the melody comfortably. And don't worry about getting all the notes and rhythms right!

Words: Joseph Naytowhow and Cheryl L'Hirondelle, 2000
Music: Joseph Naytowhow, 2000
Words copyright © 2000 by Joseph Naytowhow and Cheryl L'Hirondelle. Used by permission.
Music copyright © 2000 by Joseph Naytowhow. Used by permission.

142

Oh a Song Must Rise
(A Song Must Rise)

Swing Refrain

♩ = 132

Oh a song must rise for the spir-it to des-cend

Oh a song must rise once a-gain (a-

gain) Sing-ing out God's prai-ses and glo-ry, the faith-ful voi-ces blend,

Oh a song must rise for the spir-it to des-cend. (des-cend)

Fine

Words and music: Paul B. Svenson, 1995; arr. Bryn Nixon, 2006
Words and music copyright © 1995 Paul B. Svenson, Dad's Songbook Music, www.dadsongbook.com
Used by permission.
Arrangement copyright © 2006 Bryn Nixon. Used by permission.

143   We Cannot Own the Sunlit Sky
(Abundant Life)

1 We can-not own the sun-lit sky,   the
2 When bod-ies shiv-er in the night   and
3 God calls hu-man-i-ty to join   as

moon, the wild-flow'rs grow-ing,   for we are
wea - ry, wait for morn-ing,   when chil - dren
part - ners in cre - at - ing   a fu - ture

part of all that is with - in life's riv - er
have no bread but tears, and war - horns sound their
free from want or fear, life's good - ness cel - e -

flow - ing.   With o - pen
warn - ing,   God calls hu -
brat - ing,   that new world

Words: Ruth Duck
Music: Marty Haugen
Words and music copyright © by GIA Publications, Inc. All rights reserved.
7404 S. Mason Ave., Chicago, IL 60638. www.giamusic.com.
800-442-1358. Used by permission.

LA GRANGE
8 7 8 7 D
Alternate tune: MEGERRAN or
HOW CAN I KEEP FROM SINGING

144   Like a Healing Stream

1 Like a heal-ing stream   in   a   bar - ren
2 Like a gen - tle rain   on   a thirs - ty
3 Like a ri - ver strong   with   a rest - less
4 Like a migh-ty sea   reach - ing far hor-

des - ert,   Spir - it   wat - er bring-ing life   to   dus - ty
gar - den,   Spir - it   wat - er come to nour - ish ti - ny
cur - rent,   Spir - it   wat - er rush-ing on   to   dis - tant
i - zons,   Spir - it   wat - er with a love   both deep and

earth,   God is trick - ling through our lives   as   in   a
seed,   God is bub - bling through the soil   to coax   a
shore,   God is carv - ing   out   a   chan - nel in   a
wide,   God is work - ing   in   our hearts   to shape a

dream un - fold - ing,   pro - mis-ing re - viv - al and re -
new cre - a - tion,   yearn-ing for an end   to want and
new dir - ec - tion,   call - ing for an end   to hate and
new to - mor - row: God will al ways chal - lenge and pro-

birth...   like a heal - ing stream.
need...   like a gen - tle rain.
war...   like a riv - er strong.
vide!   Like a migh - ty   sea,   like a ri-ver

strong,   like a gen - tle rain,   like a heal - ing stream.

Words and music: Bruce Harding, 2003
Words and music copyright © 2003 by Bruce Harding, www.evensong.ca. Used by permission.

145 Draw the Circle Wide

(Traçons un grand cercle)

Draw the cir-cle wide. Draw it wid-er still.

Let this be our song, no one stands a-lone, stand-ing side by side,

draw the cir-cle wide.

1 God the still-point of the cir-cle, 'round whom all cre-
2 Let our hearts touch far hor-i-zons, so en-com-pass
3 Let the dreams we dream be larg-er, than we've ev-er

a-tion turns; noth-ing lost, but held for-e-ver,
great and small; let our lov-ing know no bor-ders,
dreamed be-fore; let the dream of Christ be in us,

in God's grac-ious arms.
faith-ful to God's call.
o - pen ev - ery door.

French:

Refrain
Tra-çons un grand cercle.
Tra-çons le plus grand.
C'est no-tre seul chant,
nul n'est so-li-taire,
de-bout so-li-daires,
tra-çons un grand cercle.

1. Dieu est le centre de no-tre cercle,
   tour-nent la terre et les cieux.
   Nous se-rons tou-jours à l'a-bri
   dans les bras de Dieu.

2. Que nos cœurs touchent les ho-ri-zons,
   en-ve-lop-pant cha-que lieu ;
   notre a-mour sans fin ré-pon-dra
   à l'ap-pel de Dieu.

3. Que tous nos rêves s'é-pa-nou-issent
   plus que nos rê-ves pas-sés,
   car le rê-ve de Christ en nous
   est à par-ta-ger.

Words and music: Gordon Light, 1994; arrangement: Michael Bloss, 1998; French translation: Denise Soulodre, 2006
Words and music copyright © 1994 Common Cup Company, www.commoncup.com. Used by permission.
Arrangement copyright © 1998 Wood Lake Books.
French translation copyright © 2006 by Denise Soulodre. Used by permission.

The Kingdom of God 146

The king-dom of God is jus-tice and peace and joy in the Ho-ly
Spir - it. Come, Lord*, and o-pen in us the gates of your king-dom.

* alternative: "God"

Words and music: Taizé Community
Words and music copyright © 2001 Ateliers et Presses de Taizé (France). All rights reserved. Published and printed through exclusive license
agreement by GIA Publications, Inc., 7404 S. Mason Ave.. Chicago, IL 60638. www.giamusic.com. 800-442-1358. Used by permission.

147 God, Help Us to Treasure
(Moments of Mys'try)

1 God, help us to trea - sure these mo-ments of mys - t'ry; to
2 God, help us to hon - our your pre-sence a - mong us in
3 God, help us to va - lue each mo-ment of won - der when

hal - low the Sa - cred in all that we do. Through-out ev - 'ry
new - born, in el - der, in fam - 'ly in need. By shar - ing with
peace shall o'er - sha-dow our sor - row and pain. In times shared at

sea - son may we be your a - gents of love, joy, and
oth - ers we soon will dis - co - ver your kind-ness and
Ta - ble with all who are kin - dred, may we find the

bles - sing as hearts are re - newed.
lov - ing in gen - er - ous deeds.
heal - ing to sing Love's re - frain.

A hymn celebrating "God with us" at Christmastime and throughout the year.

Words: John Oldham, 1998
Music: Lori Erhardt, 1998; arr. Bruce Harding, 2006
Words copyright © 2002 by John Wesley Oldham. Used by permission.
Music copyright © Lori L. Erhardt, Box 443, Oxbow, SK S0C 2B0. Email – bigdog.farm@sasktel.net. Used by permission.
Arrangement copyright © .

Hope of Abraham and Sarah

148

1 Hope of A-bra-ham and Sar-ah, friend of Ha-gar, God of Ruth,
2 Root us in our own tra-di-tion, faith our fore-bears han-ded down.
3 Hope of A-bra-ham and Sar-ah, sov-'reign God whom we a-dore,

you de-sire that ev-'ry peo-ple wor-ship you in spir-it, truth.
Grow us in your grace and know-ledge; plant our feet on so-lid ground.
form in us your new cre-a-tion free of vio-lence, hate, and war.

Meet us in our sac-red plac-es, mosque and syn-a-gogue and church.
Cul-ti-vate the seeds of shar-ing in this world of ma-ny creeds.
So may To-rah, cross and cres-cent, each a sign of life made new,

Show us paths of un-der-stand-ing; bless us in our com-mon search.
Keep us o-pen, wise in learn-ing, bear-ing fruit in lov-ing deeds.
point us t'ward your love and jus-tice, earth at peace and one in you.

A hymn of unity for the Abrahamic traditions; Islam, Judaism, and Christianity.

Words: Ruth Duck, 2004
Music: Judith Snowdon, 2006

CAELAN
8 7 8 7 D
Alternate tunes: OMNI DIE
or ARFON (major)

Words copyright © 2005 by GIA Publications, Inc. All rights reserved. 7404 S. Mason Ave., Chicago, IL 60638.
www.giamusic.com. 800-442-1358. Used by permission.
Music copyright © 2006 by Judith Snowdon. Used by permission.

149 Peace for the Children

Unison
♩ = 88

1 Peace for the chil-dren, peace peace.
Peace for the chil-dren we pray. Fol-low-ing the path of
One of peace, we work for heal-ing, we
work for peace; peace for the chil-dren to - day.

2. Peace for the women...
3. Peace for the men...
4. Peace in our families...
5. Peace for the nations...
6. Peace for the creatures...
7. Peace for our planet...

8. Peace in the universe...
9. *Hum this verse softly, during which time individuals may call out the word "peace" in other languages, making a global connection.*
10. Peace in the soul...

Words and music: Doreen Lankshear-Smith, 1993; arr. David Abramsky, 1998
Words and music copyright © 1993 Doreen Lankshear-Smith. rellolovers@hotmail.com. Used by permission.
Arrangement copyright © 1998 David Abramsky. Used by permission.

Spirit God, Be Our Breath
(Embracing Change)

150

Words and music: Bruce Harding, 1997
Words and music copyright © 1997 by Bruce Harding, www.evensong.ca. Used by permission.

151 Your Will Be Done
(Mayenziwe)

Xhosa pronunciation: *Mah-yay-nzee-way ntah-ndoh yah-khoh.*

Words and music: traditional song, South Africa, as taught by George A. Mxadana; English trans. George A Mxadana; French trans. Paul-Jean Olangi
Music, English and french translations copyright © 1996 General Board of Global Ministries, GBG Musik, 475 Riverside Dr., New York, NY 10115.
All rights reserved. Used by permission.

You Who Watch the Highest Heavens 152
(Song of Sanctuary)

1 You who watch the high - est hea - vens wond-'ring where God's
2 You who build ex - o - tic build - ings tall - er than the
3 You who tra - vel Earth as pil - grims, dream - ing where you'd
4 You who hope for joys in hea - ven, do you know the

man-sions are; you who hope to spot an an - gel
for - est tree, don't you know that all foun - da - tions
rath - er be; God's own glo - ry fills my bo - dy,
joys of Earth? An - cient for - ests filled with sing - ing,

spin-ning like a fal - ling star; Earth is call - ing,
deep, deep down re - side in me? Earth is call - ing,
I am God's own sanc - tu - ary. Earth is call - ing,
seas that shout when whales give birth? Earth is call - ing,

come back home and rest in me.
come back home and live in me.
come back home to God in me.
come back home and sing with me.

Words: Norman Habel, 2000
Music: Neil Weisensel, 2006

LANDRECHT
878747

Words copyright © 2000 Norman Habel. Administered by Willow Publishing Pty. Ltd. All rights reserved. Used by permission.
Music copyright © 2006 Neil Weisensel. SOCAN. www.neilmusic.com. Used by permission.

153   Body, Mind and Spirit

1 Bo - dy, mind and spir - it, ho - ly, earth - ly trin - i - ty, joy of God, Cre - a - tor, life lived a - bun - dant - ly.

2 Bo - dy, mind and spir - it, chal - lenged, bat - tered by earth's ills, know that Christ rests with in us, and storm - y wat - er stills.

3 Bo - dy, mind and spir - it, nur - tured in com - mun - i - ty, prayer, con - cern, lov - ing ac - tion, faith - ful hu - man - i - ty.

4 Bo - dy, mind and spir - it, in God's im - age born to be. Sing, re - joice in life most sa - cred. Re - vel in mys - ter - y.

Words and music: Margaret Motum
Words and music copyright © Margaret Motum, 470 Wickham St., Oshawa, ON L1K 1R9. Used by permission.

PARISH NURSING
irregular

Deep in Our Hearts

1 Deep in our hearts there is a com-mon vis - ion;
2 Deep in our hearts there is a com-mon pur - pose;
3 Deep in our hearts there is a com-mon long - ing;
4 Deep in our hearts there is a com-mon vis - ion;

deep in our hearts there is a com-mon song;
deep in our hearts there is a com-mon goal;
deep in our hearts there is a com-mon theme;
deep in our hearts there is a com-mon song;

deep in our hearts there is a com-mon sto - ry,
deep in our hearts there is a sa - cred mes - sage,
deep in our hearts there is a com-mon cur - rent,
deep in our hearts there is a com-mon sto - ry,

tell-ing Cre - a - tion that we are one.
jus-tice and peace in har - mo - ny.
flow-ing to free - dom like a stream.
tell-ing Cre - a - tion that we are one.

Words: John Oldham, 1995
Music: Ron Klusmeier, 1996
Words copyright © 1995 by John Wesley Oldham. Used by permission.
Music copyright © 1996 by Ron Klusmeier, www.musiklus.com. Used by permission.

FREED
11 10 11 9

155 Unbounded Spirit, Breath of God

♩ = 108

1 Un - bound - ed Spir - it, breath of God, re-fresh-ing wa - ter,
2 Re - ceive and o - pen for re - view the work we do, the
3 Un - cov - er all the hope - less ways we run, re - sist, re-
4 As - sem - ble, leav - en, mix, and knead our clash - ing norms, op-
5 In - scribe on e - very grow - ing skill, on e - very ac - tion,

cleans - ing flame, we give al - le - giance, through your
word we preach, and school us, as we teach and
bel, or hide. Un - wrap with love and bathe in
pos - ing views and bake a loaf of joy and
e - very vow, the liv - ing name of Je - sus

call, to Christ, and to no oth - er name.
learn, in care - ful thought and truth - ful speech.
light our pain, our sad - ness, and our pride.
peace that hun - gry hearts will not re - fuse.
Christ, be - gin - ning here, be - gin - ning now.

A hymn written for the 150th anniversary of Chicago Theological Seminary.

Words: Brian Wren, 2004
Music: Jane Best, 2006
Words copyright © 2004 Hope Publishing Company, Carol Stream, IL 60188. Used by permission.
Music copyright © 2006 Jane Best. jane@bestsongs.ca. Used by permission.

PARTRIDGE
8 8 8 8
Alternate tune: WINCHESTER NEW

Dance with the Spirit

* **alternatives:** "move" or "sing"

From the Strathdee "Mass for the Healing of the Earth," this shorter song celebrates the presence and prodding of the Holy Spirit.

Words and music: Jim Strathdee, 1995
Words and music copyright © 1995 by Jim and Jean Strathdee (Desert Flower Music), PO Box 1476, Carmichael, CA 95609l (916) 481-2999.
www.strathdeemusic.com Used by permission.

157   I Am a Child of God

Unison

♩ = 152

1 I am a child of God, I am a glimpse of God's
2 I am an end - less prayer, I am a yearn-ing for
3 I am an ang - ry voice, I am com - pas - sion and
4 I am a cry for peace, I am com - mit-ment and
5 I am a song of joy, I am the mo-ment of

new cre - a - tion. I am a child of
con - temp - la - tion, I am an end - less
con - stern - a - tion, I am an ang - ry
ded - i - ca - tion, I am a cry for
ju - bi - la - tion, I am a song of

God, I am a child of God.
prayer, I am an end - less prayer.
voice, I am an ang - ry voice.
peace, I am a cry for peace.
joy, I am a song of joy.

This song may be sung as a unison hymn or as a round with entries as indicated by the numbers above the staff.

Words and music: Cheryl and Bruce Harding, 2002
Words and music copyright © 2002 by Cheryl and Bruce Harding, www.evensong.ca. Used by permission.

Dream a Dream

Words: Shirley Erena Murray, 1996
Music: Ron Klusmeier, 2005
Words copyright © 1997 by Hope Publishing Company, Carol Stream, IL 60188. All rights reserved. Used by permission.
Music copyright © 2005 by Ron Klusmeier, www.musiklus.com. Used by permission.

159 In Star and Crescent

1 In star and cres-cent, wheel and flame, in rug-ged cross and
2 In burn-ing in-cense, tith-ing gifts, in break-ing bread and
3 With var-ied hopes and dreams and creeds, all tiles in one mo-

emp-ty tomb, we im-age forth one match-less name,
pour-ing wine, each act of ar-dent wor-ship lifts
sa-ic whole, we serve our God in faith-ful deeds

one ho-ly ma-trix, fount, and womb. Though dif-ferent cul-tures
our hu-man hearts to Love Di-vine. In Bud-dhist chant and
on path-ways to one com-mon goal. No Jew nor Gen-tile,

tribes, and lands use lens-es ground to dif-fering sight,
Mus-lim prayer, in sho-far, drum, and sac-red song,
slave nor free, no male and fe-male set a-part,

A hymn celebrating the gifts and common goals of many faith traditions.

Words: Mary Louise Bringle, 2001
Music: Jane Best, 2006
AMITY
8 8 8 8 D
Alternate tune: CANDLER

Words copyright © 2002 by GIA Publications, Inc. All rights reserved. 7404 S. Mason Ave., Chicago, IL 60638.
www.giamusic.com. 800-442-1358. Used by permission.
Music copyright © 2006 Jane Best. jane@bestsongs.ca. Used by permission.

each co - lour of the pri - sm's bands re -
the mu - sic thank - ful spir - its share give
but all are one, as fa - mi - ly held

fracts from one all - daz - zling light.
praise in voi - ces mil - lions strong.
close with - in our Ma - ker's heart.

There's a River of Life 160
(River of Life)

Unison
♩ = 120

There's a ri - ver of life that's flow-ing from His* throne, a ri - ver of

life that's flow-ing from His* throne. Won't you come on in and see? This

ri - ver will set you free! Way yah hey yah, way yah hey yah, high yah way.

* alternative: "God's throne"

This song from a Canadian Mohawk composer is meant to be sung in unison, without chordal accompaniment, in as high a key as is comfortable for your group. A simple unaccented quarter-note drum and shaker accompaniment will help drive the rhythm of the song. The non-English syllables are vocables, intended as vehicles for untexted praise.

Words and music: Jonathan Maracle
Words and music copyright © by Jonathan Maracle. SOCAN. All rights reserved. www.brokenwalls.com. Used by permission.

161 I Have Called You by Your Name
(Tu sais...je t'ai appelé(e) par ton nom)

1 I have called you by your name, you are mine;
2 I will help you learn my name as you go;
3 I know you will need my touch as you go;
4 I have giv-en you a name, it is mine;

I have gift-ed you and ask you now to shine.
read it writ-ten in my peo-ple, help them grow.
feel it puls-ing in cre-a-tion's ebb and flow.
I have giv-en you my Spir-it as a sign.

I will not a-ban-don you; all my prom-is-es are
Pour the wa-ter in my name, speak the word your soul can
Like the wo-man reach-ing out, choos-ing faith in spite of
With my won-der in your soul, make my wound-ed chil-dren

true. You are gift-ed, called, and chos-en; you are mine.
claim, of-fer Je-sus' bod-y giv-en long a-go.
doubt, hold the hem of Je-sus' robe, then let it go.
whole; go and tell my prec-ious peo-ple they are mine.

A hymn for ordination, commitment, and commissioning.

Words and music: Daniel Charles Damon, 1995; French trans. David Fines, 2006
Words and music copyright © 1995 Hope Publishing Company, Carol Stream, IL 60188. All rights reserved. Used by permission.
French translation copyright © 2006 David Fines. Used by permission.

KELLY
10 11 7 7 11

French translation for #161:

1. Tu sais...je t'ai ap-pe-lé(e) par ton nom;
   au-jour-d'hui, pour moi, ra-yon-ne de
   tes dons.
   Je te gar-de près de moi;
   mes pro-mes-ses sont pour toi.
   Je t'ai choi-si(e) et ap-pe-lé(e) par
   ton nom.

2. Je t'ap-pren-drai mon nom à cha-que pas.
   Lis-le en tous ceux que tu ren-con-
   tre-ras.
   En ver-sant l'eau en mon nom,
   proc-cla-me la com-mu-nion;
   et de Jé-sus, qui s'est don-né,
   suis les pas.

3. Tu au-ras be-soin de moi en che-min.
   En tous lieux, sens ma pré-sence et
   mon sou-tien.
   Com-me cet-te femme en pleurs
   qui a surmonté ses peurs,
   touche et laisse aller Jé-sus sur
   son che-min.

4. Je t'ai don-né un nom qui est le mien.
   Main-te-nant, par mon Es-prit,
   tu m'ap-par-tiens.
   Par mon nom l'âme a-ni-mée,
   gué-ris mes en-fants bles-sés.
   Va, dis-leur qu'ils me sont pré-cieux,
   qu'ils sont miens.

Christ, within Us Hidden   162

A hymn based on the work of Australian cartoonist and writer Michael Leunig. "That which is Christ-like within us shall be crucified. It shall suffer and be broken. And that which is Christ-like within us shall rise up. It shall love and create." – (from A Common Prayer, *Michael Leunig, 1990)*

Words: S. Curtis Tufts, 2005
Music: Sid Woolfrey, 2005; arrangement: Bruce Harding, 2005
Words copyright © 2005 by S. Curtis Tufts – 178 Greenwood Drive, Spruce Grove, AB T7X 1Y7. Used by permission.
Music copyright © 2005 by Sid Woolfrey, NL. Used by permission. Arrangement copyright © .

ALEXANDER
6565
Alternate tune:
ERNSTEIN

163 River Running in You and Me
(River Run Deep)

1 Riv - er run-ning in you and me, Spir-it of life, deep
2 Riv - er laughed on my birth-ing day, Wind and wat-er
3 Ri - ver, cry my name to me, lend me hope and

mys-ter - y, danc - ing down to the ho - ly sea,
joined in play soaked my soul in a shin-ing spray,
mem-o-ry, sing me the sto-ry of the ho - ly sea,

Riv - er run deep, Riv - er run
Riv - er run deep, Riv - er run
Riv - er run deep, Riv - er run

Words and music: Ian Macdonald and Gordon Light, 2003; arr. Andrew Donaldson
Words and music copyright © 2003 Common Cup Company, www.commoncup.com. Used by permission.
Arrangement copyright © Andrew Donaldson. Used by permission.

4. I stand on the edge, look-in' down,
   too scared to swim, a-fraid I'll drown –
   give me the cour-age to jour-ney on,
   Riv-er run deep, Riv-er run free.

5. Jour-ney on far from my home,
   Riv-er – break this heart of stone;
   teach me to love, make me your own,
   Riv-er run deep, Riv-er run free.

6. Hold me close on the day I die,
   bear me up when my soul is tired,
   car-ry me home on the ris-ing tide,
   Riv-er run deep, Riv-er run free.

7. Riv-er sing-in' in you and me,
   Spir-it of life – deep mys-ter-y –
   catch us up in your mel-o-dy
   Riv-er run deep, Riv-er run free.

Christe, Lux Mundi 164

Translation: O Christ, light of the world, whoever follows you will have the light of life.

Words and music: Taizé Community
Words and music copyright © Taizé Community, France, admin. GIA Publications, Inc., excl. N. American agent.
All rights reserved. Used by permission.

165 There Is a Time

Unison
♩ = 100

D   Bm

1 There is a time that we must rise
2 There is a time that we must leave
3 There is a time we know the way
4 Up - on the dry a cloud will rise
5 There is a bow with - in the rain

Em   G/A

There is a time that we must stand
Go from the place where ha - treds breed
There is a time we watch and pray
And truth will shine a - mong the lies
And it will come and bend a - gain

A[7]   F#m   Harmony   Bm[7]   Dmaj[7]/A

There is a time that we must come (come) to -
and, turn - ing, feel the Spir - it breathe (breathe) us to -
In liv - ing faith we make our way (way) to -
And wis - dom sing as we a - rise (rise) to -
And co - lours shine where we have been (been) to -

G   Em   Aadd[2]   D   G   A

ge - ther (to - ge - ther) For bless - ed are our

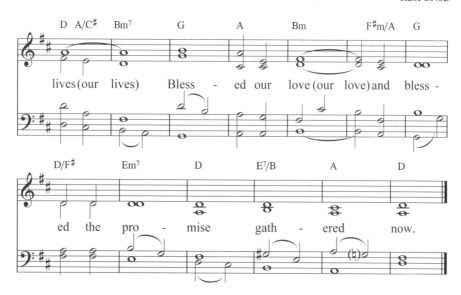

lives (our lives) Bless - ed our love (our love) and bless -

ed the pro - mise gath - ered now.

In the unison verses, the alto line may be sung as an echo of the melody.

Words and music: Carolyn McDade   Arrangement: Lydia Pedersen, 2006
Words and music copyright © Carolyn McDade Music. www.gis.net/~surtsey/mcdade. Email: surtsey@gis.net. Used by permission.
Arrangement copyright © 2006 by Lydia Pedersen. Used by permission.

Jesus Christ, Jesus Christ ## 166

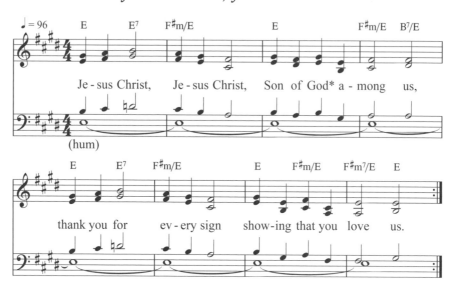

Je - sus Christ, Je - sus Christ, Son of God* a - mong us,

(hum)

thank you for ev - ery sign show-ing that you love us.

* alternatives: "Child of Earth," "Word made Flesh"

This versatile song can be a prayer or scripture response.

Words and music: John L. Bell, 1998
Words and music copyright © 1998 by WGRG, Iona Community, Scotland, admin. GIA Publications, Inc., excl. N. American agent.
All rights reserved. Used by permission.

167

Hush! Hush!

oh mah Lawd*, what shall I do? (What shall I do?)

mah Lawd*, mah Lawd*,

* alternative: "my Lord" or "my God"

The arranger, Stephen Lee, an African-American composer and scholar of African-American spirituals, asked that the dialect English be used to invite people to sing in a more authentic style. The rhythmic style of the song should be a 12/8 swing, as in this example:

Hush!   Hush!   *simile*

Hush,   all God's chil - dren. Hush,   won't   you lis - ten

Words and music: African-American spiritual; arr. Stephen Lee, 2006
Arrangement copyright © 2006 Professional Music Services. Used by permission.

May Peace Be with You   168
(Salamun, Kullaheen)

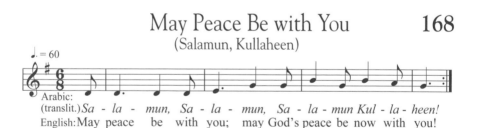

♩. = 60

Arabic:
(translit.) *Sa - la - mun, Sa - la - mun, Sa - la - mun Kul - la - heen!*
English: May peace be with you; may God's peace be now with you!

A traditional blessing. **Arabic pronunciation:** *Sah-lah-moon koo-lah-heen*

Words: author unknown; English para. S T Kimbrough, Jr.
Music: traditional melody, Lebanon
English paraphrase copyright © 2004 General Board of Global Ministries, GBGMusik, 475 Riverside Dr., New York, NY 10115. All rights reserved. Used by permission.

169 When Hands Reach Out Beyond Divides

♩ = 132

1 When hands reach out be - yond di - vides and
2 When fear no long - er guides our steps and
3 When race and creed blind us no more, a

hope is tru - ly found, each chain of hate will
days of war are done, God's dream for all shall
neigh - bour's face we'll see, and we shall dance the

fall a - way and bells of peace shall sound, and
live a - new; our hearts will heal as one, our
whole world round, for love will set us free, for

bells of peace, of peace shall sound, and bells of peace shall
hearts will heal, will heal as one, our hearts will heal as
love, yes love will set us free, for love will set us

Words: Keri K. Wehlander, 2005
Music: Composer unknown, from *Southern Harmony*, 1854 edition;
arr. Melva Treffinger Graham, 2006
Words copyright © 2005 by Keri K. Wehlander, www.creativeworship.ca.
Used by permission.
Arrangement copyright © 2006 by Melva Treffinger Graham. Used by permission.

SALEM
8 6 8 6 D
Alternate tune: FOREST GREEN or KINGSFOLD

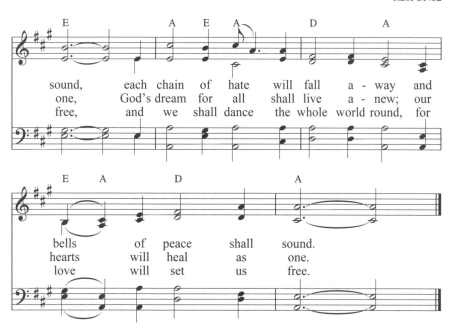

sound,   each chain of hate   will fall   a - way   and
one,   God's dream for all   shall live   a - new;   our
free,   and   we   shall dance   the whole world round,   for

bells   of   peace   shall   sound.
hearts   will   heal   as   one.
love   will   set   us   free.

Ubi Caritas 170
(Where There Is Charity)

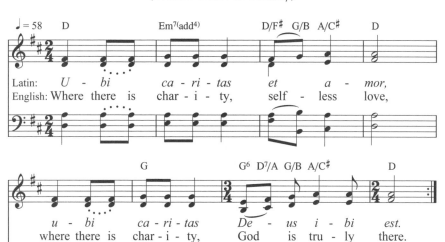

Latin: U - bi   ca - ri - tas   et   a - mor,
English: Where there is   char - i - ty,   self - less   love,

u - bi   ca - ri - tas   De - us   i - bi   est.
where there is   char - i - ty,   God   is   tru - ly   there.

These words, from the antiphon for the ceremony of the Washing of the Feet on Maundy Thursday, are also suitable for communion and general use.

Words: Taizé Community
Music: Joseph Gelineau

Words and music copyright © 1998 Taizé Community, France, admin. GIA Publications, Inc., excl. N. American agent.
All rights reserved. Used by permission.

171 Christ Has No Body Now but Yours

Refrain

Christ has no bo-dy now but yours, no hands but yours. Here on this earth, yours is the work, to serve with the joy of com-pas - sion.

1 No hands but yours to heal the wound-ed world,
2 No eyes but yours to see as Christ would see,
3 No feet but yours to jour-ney with the poor,
4 Through ev - 'ry gift, give back to those in need:

no hands but yours to soothe all its suf-fering, no touch but yours to
to find the lost, to gaze with com-pas-sion; no eyes but yours to
to walk this world with mer - cy and jus - tice. Yours are the steps to
as Christ has blessed, so now be his bless-ing, with ev - 'ry gift a

Words: Adapted by Stephen C. Warner, 2003, from St. Teresa of Avila
Music: Rick Gunn, 2006
Words copyright © 2003, World Library Publications, 3708 River Rd., Suite 400, Franklin Park, IL 60131-2158. 800-566-6150. www.wlpmusic.com.
All rights reserved. Used by permission.
Music copyright copyright © 2006 by Rick Gunn, www.rickgunn.com. Used by permission.

Em   Am⁷   D⁷   D.C.

bind   the   bro - ken hope   of   the   peo   -   ple   of   God.
glimpse the   ho - ly   joy   of   the   ci   -   ty   of   God.
build   a   last - ing peace for the   chil   -   dren   of   God.
ben - e - dic - tion,   be   to   the   peo   -   ple   of   God.

God Says   172

Unison
♩ = 72

F   B♭

1 God   says, "Be   still   so   you may   hear   the words I
2 God   says, "Look up   and   see   the   prize   I've placed here
3 God   says, "Come here!   I   need your voice. Please teach my
4 God   says, "Reach out! The world's in   need   and wants a

Gm   C   Am   A⁷/C♯

whis - per   in your   ear.   If you will   lis   -   ten, you will
right   be - fore your eyes. Find beau - ty   in   the things of
peo - ple   to   re - joice.   In who you   are,   in what you
word,   a   song, a   deed.   I send you   forth   to speak, to

Dm   B♭   C⁷   F

know   I'm   with   you   al - ways   where you   go."
earth,   a   cause for   won - der   and re - birth."
do,   your life will   show   my   love for   you."
sing,   to   act for   Christ   in   ev - ery - thing."

Words and music: Mary Bittner, 1993
Words and music copyright © 2004 by Wayne Leupold Editions, Inc. Used by permission.

GOD SAYS
8 8 8 8
Alternate tunes: O WALY WALY or TALLIS' CANON

173 Put Peace into Each Other's Hands
(Hands Shaped Like a Cradle)

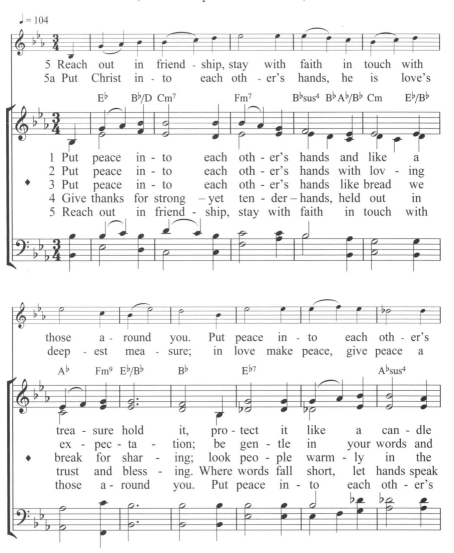

5 Reach out in friend - ship, stay with faith in touch with
5a Put Christ in - to each oth - er's hands, he is love's

1 Put peace in - to each oth - er's hands and like a
2 Put peace in - to each oth - er's hands with lov - ing
3 Put peace in - to each oth - er's hands like bread we
4 Give thanks for strong – yet ten - der – hands, held out in
5 Reach out in friend - ship, stay with faith in touch with

those a - round you. Put peace in - to each oth - er's
deep - est mea - sure; in love make peace, give peace a

trea - sure hold it, pro - tect it like a can - dle
ex - pec - ta - tion; be gen - tle in your words and
break for shar - ing; look peo - ple warm - ly in the
trust and bless - ing. Where words fall short, let hands speak
those a - round you. Put peace in - to each oth - er's

A hymn for interfaith worship or for communion.

Words: Fred Kaan, 1989, rev. 2001
Music: Ron Klusmeier, 2004
Words and music copyright © 2004 Hope Publishing Company, Carol Stream, IL 60188. All rights reserved. Used by permission.

hands: the Peace that sought and found you.
chance, and share it like a trea - sure.

flame, with ten - der - ness en - fold it.
ways, in touch with God's cre - a - tion.
◆ eye: our life is meant for car - ing.
out, the heights of love ex - press - ing.
hands; the Peace that sought and found you.

Alternate 4th and 5th verses for communion:

4a. As at com-mu-nion, shape your hands
into a wait-ing cra-dle;
the gift of Christ re-ceive, re-vere,
u-ni-ted round the ta-ble.

5a. Put Christ in-to each oth-er's hands,
he is love's deep-est mea-sure;
in love make peace, give peace a chance,
and share it like a trea-sure.

174

Soil of God, You and I
(Holy Ground)

♩ = 100

1 Soil of God, you and I, stand read-y to bear seeds of faith
2 Soil of God, you and I, now read-y to be part of God's
3 Soil of God, you and I, now called to re - birth, join-ing as

nour-ished by God's ten-der care. Grow-ing in eve-ry-one for
pro - mise, for oth-ers to see. O - pen to eve-ry-one for
part - ners with all of the earth. Liv - ing in har-mo-ny for

here God is found. All stand to - ge-ther, we are...
here God is found. All stand to - ge-ther, we are...
here God is found. All stand to - ge-ther, this is...

Words and music: jim hannah, 1995; arr. David Melhorn-Boe, 2006
Words and music copyright © 1995 jim hannah. Used by permission.
Arrangement copyright © 2006 David Melhorn-Boe, 238 First Ave. E., North Bay, ON P1B 1J8. email: mboe@onlink.net.

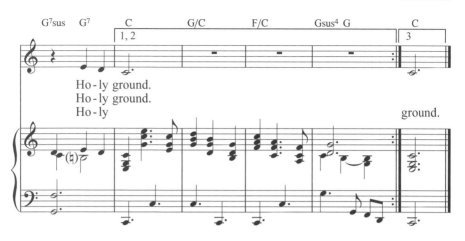

Ho-ly ground.
Ho-ly ground.
Ho-ly
ground.

May We but Wait

175

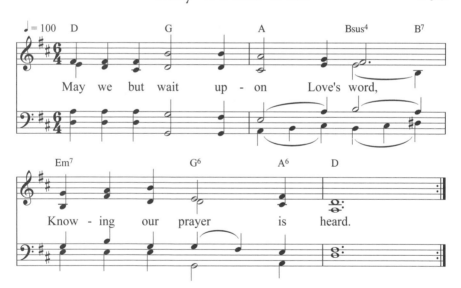

May we but wait up - on Love's word,

Know - ing our prayer is heard.

A prayer response, discernment song, or prayer for illumination.

Words and music: Will Petricko, 2004
Words and music copyright © 2004 by William B. Petricko. songwriter@canada.com. Used by permission.

176 Three Things I Promise
(Ce que je promets)

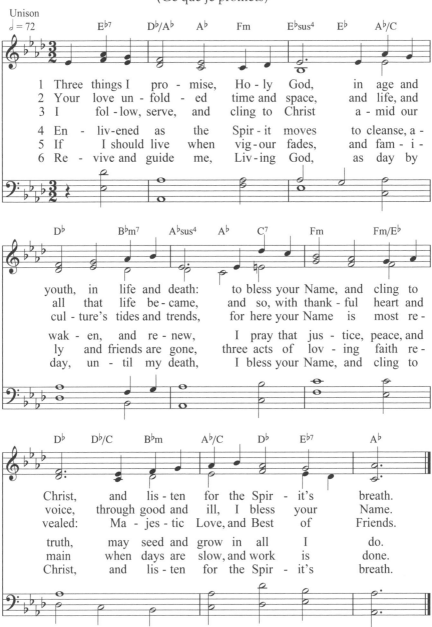

Unison ♩ = 72

1 Three things I pro-mise, Ho-ly God, in age and
2 Your love un-fold-ed time and space, and life, and
3 I fol-low, serve, and cling to Christ a-mid our
4 En-liv-ened as the Spir-it moves to cleanse, a-
5 If I should live when vig-our fades, and fam-i-
6 Re-vive and guide me, Liv-ing God, as day by

youth, in life and death: to bless your Name, and cling to
all that life be-came, and so, with thank-ful heart and
cul-ture's tides and trends, for here your Name is most re-
wak-en, and re-new, I pray that jus-tice, peace, and
ly and friends are gone, three acts of lov-ing faith re-
day, un-til my death, I bless your Name, and cling to

Christ, and lis-ten for the Spir-it's breath.
voice, through good and ill, I bless your Name.
vealed: Ma-jes-tic Love, and Best of Friends.
truth, may seed and grow in all I do.
main when days are slow, and work is done.
Christ, and lis-ten for the Spir-it's breath.

Words: Brian Wren, 1997; French trans. David Fines, 2006
Music: Daniel Charles Damon, 1999
Words copyright © 1997 and music copyright © 1999 Hope Publishing Company, Carol Stream, IL 60188.
All rights reserved. Used by permission.
French translation copyright © 2006 David Fines. Used by permission.

BLANN
8 8 8 8
Alternate tunes: WAREHAM
or PROSPECT

French translation for #176:

1. Ce que je pro-mets, ô Dieu saint,
   c'est d'être à toi dès au-jour-d'hui,
   chan-ter pour toi cha-que ma-tin,
   d'être à l'é-cou-te de l'Es-prit.

2. Ton a-mour a cré-é le temps,
   cré-é l'u-ni-vers et la vie;
   ain-si mon cœur re-con-nais-sant,
   Dieu, te rend grâce et te bé-nit.

3. Je veux ser-vir, sui-vre Jé-sus
   que ce soit loin ou bien i-ci;
   son nom nous of-fre le sa-lut.
   Ma-jes-té, A-mour, Tendre A-mi.

4. Par ton Es-prit-Saint, a-ni-mé,
   pour gué-rir et re-nou-ve-ler,
   que paix, jus-tice et vé-ri-té,
   ger-ment de tout ce que je fais.

5. Quand j'au-rai at-teint les vieux jours,
   que se-ront par-tis mes a-mis,
   ce que j'ai pro-mis dans l'a-mour
   se-ra comme un der-nier mer-ci.

6. Oui, gar-de-moi, ô Dieu vi-vant,
   en cha-que ma-tin de ma vie ;
   que jus-qu'au der-nier, con-fi-ant,
   je chante et j'é-cou-te l'Es-prit.

This Is My Body 177

Words and music: Daniel Charles Damon, 1994
Words and music copyright © 1998 Hope Publishing Company, Carol Stream, IL 60188. All rights reserved. Used by permission.

SOQUEL
5 5 4 4 5 5 7

178 Who Is My Mother
(Kindred in Spirit through Jesus Christ)

1 Who is my moth-er, who is my broth-er?
2 Dif - ferent-ly a - bled, dif ferent-ly la-belled,
3 Love will re - late us col - our or sta - tus
4 Bound by one vi - sion, met for one mis - sion

All those who gath - er round Je - sus Christ:
wid - en the cir - cle round Je - sus Christ:
can't seg - re - gate us round Je - sus Christ:
we claim each oth - er, round Je - sus Christ:

Spir - it blown peo - ple born from the Gos - pel
crutch - es and stig - mas, cul - ture's e - nig - mas,
fam - i - ly fail - ings, hu - man de - rail - ings
here is my moth - er, here is my broth - er,

sit at the ta - ble, round Je - sus
all come to - geth - er round Je - sus
all are ac - cept - ed round Je - sus
kin - dred in Spir - it, through Je - sus

Words: Shirley Erena Murray, 1992
Music: Ron Klusmeier, 2002
Words copyright © 1992 Hope Publishing Company, Carol Stream, IL 60188. All rights reserved. Used by permission.
Music copyright © 2005 Ron Klusmeier. www.musiklus.com. Used by permission.

Christ.
Christost.
Christ.
Christ.

A-men!

Sisters Let Us Walk Together   179

Round
♩ = 100

1 Sis - ters let us walk to - geth - er, shar - ing sad - ness,
2 Broth - ers let us work to - geth - er, seek - ing jus - tice,
3 Peo - ple let us love to - geth - er, join - ing spir - its,

loss and grief, we will move through pain to whole - ness,
heal - ing shame, filled with hope, em - bued with cour - age,
link - ing hands, we are God's un - ique cre - a - tion,

brok - en - ness trans - formed to peace.
ev' - ry viol - ence we will name.
clothed with dig - ni - ty we'll stand.

Written for a worship service to honour the women killed in the Montreal Massacre of 1989, this song can be sung as a unison hymn or as a round, and can be sung using "Sisters," "Brothers," or "People" for all three verses.

Words and music: Judith Snowdon, 2004
Words and music copyright © Judith Snowdon, 2004. Used by permission.

180

Sing, Sing Out!
(Sing a New Song)

1 Sing, sing out! Sing a new song. Sing oh peo-ple as one voice! Sing, sing out! Sing a new song. Sing of God. Each heart re-joice! Sing! Hal-le-lu-jah! Hal-le-lu-jah, as one voice! Sing! Hal-le-lu-jah! Hal-le-lu-jah, all re-joice!

2 Sing, sing out! Sing a new song. Sing oh peo-ple for re-birth! Sing, sing out! Sing a new song. Sing of God in all the earth! Sing! Hal-le-lu-jah! Hal-le-lu-jah, for re-birth! Sing! Hal-le-lu-jah! Hal-le-lu-jah, all re-joice!

A rousing call to embrace the new, this song can be sung as a unison song or as a round.

Words and music: jim hannah, 2003; arr. David Melhorn-Boe, 2006
Words and music copyright © 2003 jim hannah. Used by permission.
Arrangement copyright © 2006 David Melhorn-Boe, 238 First Ave. E., North Bay, ON P1B 1J8. email: mboe@onlink.net.

Lord, Your Hands Have Formed

(Imegmoy pitak ay yay)

181

Ikalahan:
1 I - meg - moy pi - tak ay yay I - meg -
2 Pan - ta - ne - man i - pi - tak Tak - lay

English:
1 Lord*, your hands have formed this world, ev - ery
2 Yours the soil that holds the seed, you give

moh a - da - tak - lay. I - meg - moh a - da da -
i ma - ngi - to - dak; Da - nom i an ma - ni -
part is shaped by you. Wa - ter tum - bling o - ver
warmth and mois-ture, too. Sprout-ing crops and bloss - om

nom, Eg - gew tan wa - day e -
bog, Eg - gew i on da - da
rocks, air and sun - light each day's
buds, trees and plants: the sea - sons'

dom, Ga - yom ni hi - ga - mi.
od Ga - yom ni hi - ga - mi.
signs that you make all things new.
signs that you make all things new.

* alternative: "God"

3. Am-bel-at i ka-ya-bang
Tep o-bi-mi a-a-teng.
Da-kel i-day ma-nok-mi,
Tan ma-ta-bay kil-lo-mi,
Ga-yom ni hi-ga-mi.

4. Mik a-na-pay i-nom-an
Et wa-day pan-la-mo-nan.
Mok a-na-pay nem-nem-ni
Ang-gan i-day ba-hol-mi,
Ga-yom ni hi-ga-mi.

3. We search out new ground to
weed,
even moun-tain fields will do.
You up-root the tough-est sins
from our souls: both stew-ard
signs
that you make all things new.

4. Like a mat you roll out land,
space to build for us and you
earth-ly homes and in our midst,

A Filipino hymn celebrating God's goodness as expressed through the cycle of planting and harvest.

Words: Ramon and Sario Oliano, Philippines; trans. Delbert Rice
Music: GAYAM NI HI-GAMI; Ikalahan melody, Philippines
Words copyright © Ramon and Sario Oliano. Used by permission.
English translation copyright © Delbert Rice. Used by permission.

182 Grateful

Refrain

Grate-ful for the life you give us, thank-ful for your Ho-ly Son, joy-ful in your Spir-it flow-ing o-ver all, O God of Love. Grate-ful for the

Words and music: Tom Tomaszek, 2003; arr. Sarah Hart and Tom Tomaszek, 2003
Words and music copyright © 2003, Tom Tomaszek. Published by spiritandsong.com ®. All rights reserved. Used with permission.

* alternative: "Living God"

you are faith - ful to your Word.
to the glo - ry of your name.

Coda

We will praise you.

rit.

183 I'm Gonna Shout, Shout
(Shout Out Your Love)

I'm gon-na shout, shout, shout out my love for Je - sus, for Je-

sus! I'm gon-na shout, shout, shout out my love for God's

most ho- ly child! For what - ev-er I might do to-day, at

home, at school, at work, at play, I've got Je - sus' love deep

down in- side of me!

Make up additional verses and actions such as:

"I'm gonna raise, raise, raise up my hands..."
"I'm gonna dance, dance, dance all around..."

Words and music: Bruce Harding, 1998
Words and music copyright © 1998 by Bruce Harding, www.evensong.ca. Used by permission.

Ay, Ay Salidummay

184

Ay, ay sa - li-dum- may, Let us give thanks to God.

A prayer response or acclamation. The original meaning of "Salidummay" is unknown, but Christians in the Philippines have adopted the word to express the mood of joy.

Words and music: traditional song, Philippines, transcribed and adapted by I-to Loh.
Word adaptation and transcription copyright © I-to Loh. Used by permission.

185   Ev'ry Day Is a Day of Thanksgiving

Ev - 'ry day   is a day of thanks-giv-ing. God, you've been so

good to me.   Ev -'ry day you're bles-sing me.

You know that

Ev - 'ry day   is a day of thanks-giv-ing. I will glo-ri-

fy you, O my Lord*,   to - day!   (day!) You keep

Glo-ri-fy you, Lord*,

* alternative: "O my God"

A lively gospel song from the African-American tradition.

Words and music: Leonard Burks
Words and music copyright © Leonard Burks. Used by permission.

186

Because Jesus Felt

1 Be - cause Je - sus felt a wom - an touch his coat, and said,
2 Be - cause Je - sus ate with peo - ple who'd gone wrong, and said,
3 Be - cause Je - sus went to heal a lit - tle girl, and said,
4 Be - cause Je - sus sat with chil - dren on his knee, and said,
5 Be - cause Je - sus lived and died, and lives with God, and says,

"Your faith has made you well," I know that God takes no - tice, and
"You are for - giv - en now," I know that God for - gives me, and
"Get up, and have some food," I know God cares a - bout me, and
"I'm glad to meet you all," I know God thinks I'm love - ly, and
"I'm with you all the time," I know that God is near me, and

Refrain

knows my name, and loves us all:
hears my name, and loves us all: So thank you,
speaks my name, and loves us all:
sings my name, and loves us all:
calls my name, and loves us all:

thank you, God. Thank you, God!

Words: Brian Wren
Music: Daniel Charles Damon
Words and music © 1998 Hope Publishing Company, Carol Stream, IL 60188. All rights reserved. Used by permission.

OAK PARK
5 6 8 7 8 with refrain

We Give Our Thanks 187
(Reamo leboga)

Often in the African style of singing, texts are improvised. The alternate English words below are suggested improvisations by Andrew Donaldson.

We give our hands to you, (3x)
because you reached for us.

We give our feet to you, (3x)
because you walk with us.

We give our eyes to you, (3x)
because you looked for us.

We give our hearts to you, (3x)
because you first loved us.

Tswana pronunciation: *Ray-yoh-moh lay-boh-gah (the "g" in "gah" should be closer to an aspirated "h" than a "g").*

Words and music: traditional song, Botswana, as taught by Daisy Nsakazongwe
English paraphrase and transcription: I-to Loh; French trans. David Fines, 2006
Alternate English words: Andrew Donaldson

Transcription and English paraphrase copyright © 1986 World Council of Churches and the Asian Institute for Liturgy and Music. Used by permission.
French translation copyright © 2006 David Fines. Used by permission.
Textual improvisations copyright © Andrew Donaldson. Used by permission.

188 I Thank You, Thank You, Jesus
(Asante sana Yesu)

Swahili:
1 A - san - te sa - na Ye - su, a - san - te sa - na
2 Si i - shi bi - la we - we, si i - shi bi - la
3 Ni - na - ku - pen - da Ye - su, ni - na - ku - pen - da

English:
1 I thank you, thank you, Je - sus, I thank you, thank you,
2 I can't live with - out you, yes, I can't live with -
3 I love you, love you, Je - sus, I love you, love you,

Ye - su, a - san - te sa - na Ye - su mo - yo - ni.
we - we, si i - shi bi - la we - we mo - yo - ni.
Ye - su, ni - na - ku - pen - da Ye - su mo - yo - ni.

Je - sus, I thank you, thank you, Je - sus, in my heart.
out you, I can't live with - out you in my heart.
Je - sus, I love you, love you, Je - sus, in my heart.

A - san - te sa - na Ye - su, a - san - te sa - na
Si i - shi bi - la we - we, si i - shi bi - la
Ni - na - ku - pen - da Ye - su, ni - na - ku - pen - da

I thank you, thank you, Je - sus, I thank you, thank you,
I can't live with - out you, yes, I can't live with -
I love you, love you, Je - sus, I love you, love you,

A traditional song from East Africa. Harmonies for this song are best improvised – the written harmonies are only a guideline. **Swahili pronunciation:**
1. Ah-sahn-tay sah-nah Yeh-soo moh-yoh-nee.
2. See ee-shee bee-lah way-way moh-yoh-nee.
3. Nee-nah-koo-pehn-dah Yeh-soo moh-yoh-nee.

Words (Swahili) and music: traditional song, East Africa
English paraphrase and arrangement: *More Voices*, 2007
English paraphrase and arrangement copyright © 2007 The United Church of Canada.

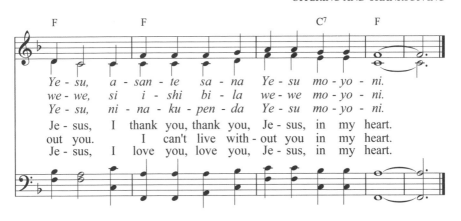

Ye - su, a - san - te sa - na Ye - su mo - yo - ni.
we - we, si i - shi bi - la we - we mo - yo - ni.
Ye - su, ni - na - ku - pen - da Ye - su mo - yo - ni.
Je - sus, I thank you, thank you, Je - sus, in my heart.
out you. I can't live with - out you in my heart.
Je - sus, I love you, love you, Je - sus, in my heart.

Jesus, We Are Here
(Jesu tawa pano)

189

Shona: Je - su ta - wa pa - no; Je - su ta - wa pa - no;
English: Je - sus, we are here; Je - sus, we are here;

Je - su ta - wa pa - no; ta - wa pa - no, mu zi - ta re - nyu.
Je - sus, we are here; we are here for you.

Try this song with shakers and other percussion.
Shona pronunciation: *Jeh-soo tah-wah pah-noh...moo-zee-tah reh-nyoo.*

Words and music: Patrick Matsikenyiri
Words and music copyright © 1990, 1996 General Board of Global Ministries, GBGMusik, 475 Riverside Drive, New York, N.Y. 10115.
All rights reserved. Used by permission.

190   Laughter Lit the Stars of Morning

Unison
♩ = 112

1 Laugh - ter   lit the stars   of morn-ing   sing - ing
2 Laugh - ter   filled a bar - ren Sar - ah: "Shall   this
3a Laugh - ter   sweeps the church   as - sem-bled   as   an
3b Laugh - ter   binds the con - gre - ga-tion   in   the

at   the dawn   of earth;   an - gel throngs re - joiced   to
an - cient womb con - ceive?   When   I feel   new life   within - fant's cry   is heard.   Oil   and wa - ter seal   the
joy   of fam - 'ly grown;   oil   and wa - ter seal   the

wit - ness   so   mi - rac - u - lous   a   birth.
in   me,   on - ly then   will   I   be - lieve!"
pro - mise   of   God's cov - e - nant - ing Word.
pro - mise   each   has made,   to   be   God's own.

As   they mar - velled at   its won - der,   teem - ing   life forms,
Sar - ah's laugh - ter turned   to won - der   at   the   thing that
Joy   and gra - ti - tude   and won - der   have   a   lov - ing
Young   and old,   we share   the won - der   of   God's co - ve-

	mul	–	ti – hued,	ten	–	der – ly	the world	God
God	had	done	when	her	long	– ing	arms	were
wel	–	come smiled,	and	our	hearts	in	un	– ion
nant	re –	newed,	our	bap	– tis	– mal	vows	re –

cra	– dled	and	pro – nounced	it	ver	–	y	good.
cra	– dling	I	– saac, her	be	– lov	–	ed	son.
cra	– dle	love	em – bo	– died,	God's	own	child.
mem	– ber,	and	give thanks,	for	God	is	good.

Verse 3a is intended for infant baptism, while verse 3b is for adult baptism and/or renewal of baptismal vows.

Words: Lydia Pedersen, 2005
Music: Ruth Watson Henderson, 2006
Words copyright © 2005 Lydia Pedersen. Used by permission.
Music copyright © 2006 Ruth Watson Henderson. Used by permission.

STARS OF MORNING
8 7 8 7 D
Alternate tune: ABBOT'S LEIGH

191 What Can I Do?

What can I do? What can I bring?
What? What can I do? What can I bring?

What can I say? What can I sing? I'll sing with
What can I say? What can I sing?

joy.(I'll sing with joy.) I'll say a prayer. I'll bring my
I'll say a prayer.

love. I'll do my share. share.
I'll bring my love. I'll do my share. share.I'll do my share.

A joyful song of offering and dedication.

Words and music: Paul Rumbolt and Michele McCarthy; arr. Alan C. Whitmore, 2005
Words and music copyright © by Paul Rumbolt and Michele McCarthy. Please visit www.paulrumbolt.com for information. Used by permission.
Arrangement copyright © 2005 Alan C. Whitmore. Used by permission.

We Come Now to Your Table Lord

We come now to your ta-ble Lord, you are the Liv-ing Bread. We
come now to your ta-ble Lord, let ev'-ry soul be fed. You
are the Liv-ing Bread, let ev'-ry soul be fed: and
now may ev'-ry soul be fed with Liv-ing Bread.

Words: Caribbean Conference of Churches Jamaica workshop
Music: traditional song, St. Vincent, adapted; arr. Patrick Prescod
Words and music copyright © Caribbean Conference of Churches. Used by permission.

193 God Bless to Us Our Bread
(Bendice, Señor, nuestro pan)

Spanish: Ben - di - ce, Se - ñor, nue-stro pan, y da pan a los que tie - nen
English: God bless to us our bread, and give bread to all those who are
French: Dieu, bé - nis no - tre pain; don-ne du pain à ceux qui ont

ham - bre y ham - bre de ju - sti - cia a los que tie -
hun - gry, and hun - ger for jus - tice to those who are
faim, don - ne faim de jus - tice à ceux qui ont du

nen; ben - di - ce, Se - ñor, nue-stro pan.
fed; God bless to us our bread.
pain; Dieu, bé - nis no - tre pain.

A grace for mealtime and communion.

Words: Bishop Federico Pagura, Argentina; English trans. John L. Bell; French trans. David Fines, 2005
Music: traditional melody, Argentina; arr. John L. Bell
Words copyright © World Council of Churches Publications, Geneva. Used by permission.
English translation and arrangement copyright © 1997, 2007 by WGRG, Iona Community, Scotland, admin. GIA Publications, Inc., excl. N. American
agent. All rights reserved. Used by permission.
French translation copyright © 2005 David Fines. Used by permission.
Music and original Spanish collected by Federico Pagura © 2002 World Council of Churches, P.O. Box 2100, CH-1211 Geneva. Used by permission.

Bread of Life, Feed My Soul

1 Bread of life, feed my soul, as the pre-sence of the Spir-
3 Bread of life, help me live a life as pure and
5 Bread of life, feed my soul, as the pre-sence of the Spir-

it makes me whole. Bread of life, fill my heart
true as Je-sus did. Bread of life, help me see
it makes me whole. Bread of life, fill my heart

with the grace and mer-cy you im-part.
the bound-less love of Christ for you and me.
with the grace and mer-cy you im - part.

Bridge

2, 4 I have heard your voice cal - ling, "Come, my friend, and share in the

feast that is laid out for you to show how much I care."

A communion prayer for healing and guidance.

Words and music: Stephen Spencer, 2005; arrangement: Rick Gunn, 2005

Words and music copyright © 2005 by Stephen Spencer, 38 Goldsboro Ave., Riverview, NB, E1B 4K4. Used by permission.
Arrangement copyright © 2005 Rick Gunn, www.rickgunn.com. Used by permission.

195 Long Ago and Far Away
(Fill the Cup)

1 Long a-go and far a-way Je-sus
2 Je-sus gath-ered the chil-dren a-round him spoke of
3 Je-sus called all his friends to be with him share the

liv-ed and worked and prayed healed the sick and the
Love and the joy to be found told them stor-ies of
bread and the cup once a-gain life to you I will

fear-ful and lone-ly lived his life to show us God's way.
wis-dom and won-der God's cre-a-tion in all that's a-round.
of-fer it glad-ly love will be with you right to the end.

Refrain

Stretched his arms out as he said Fill the cup and share the bread Re-

(after last verse repeat refrain twice)

mem-ber me in love and joy and bless - ing.

A communion song for all ages.

Words and music: Pat Mayberry, 2000; arr. Margaret Stubbington, 2006
Words and music copyright © 2000 Pat Mayberry, SOCAN. www.patmayberry.com. Used by permission.
Arrangement copyright © 2006 Margaret Stubbington. Used by permission.

We Will Take What You Offer

* **alternative: "God"**

This lively communion song or scripture response can also be a sung as a commissioning by changing the word "fed" to "led."

Words and music: John L. Bell, 1998
Words and music copyright © 1998 by WGRG, Iona Community, Scotland, admin. GIA Publications, Inc., excl. N. American agent.
All rights reserved. Used by permission.

197 Bread of Life, Broken and Shared
(Pain de vie, partagé)

Words and music: David-Roger Gagnon, 1996.
Droits d'auteur copyright © 1996 David-Roger Gagnon. Tout droits réservés. Utilisé avec permission.
Words and music copyright © 1996 David-Roger Gagnon. All rights reserved. Used with Permission.

suit n'au-ra plus ja-mais faim! Qui croit en moi n'a
brons ta ré - sur - rec - tion, Nous at - tend - ons
tombe en terre et meurt, il ne peut don -
come to me shall ne - ver hun-ger; and all who drink will
drink this sa - ving cup, we pro - claim your
to the ground and dies, it re - mains a

ja-mais soif. Je suis la vie é - ter - nelle!
ta ve - nue dans la gloi - re!
ner la vie; mais dans la mort il por - te fruit!
ne - ver thirst, for I will give e - ter - nal life!
death, un - til you come in glo - ry!
sin - gle grain, but if it dies, it bears new life!

French translation for *When We Gather at the Table*, #198:

1. Quand nous ve-nons à la ta-ble,
   le pain, le vin en par-ta-ge,
   l'a-mour est no-tre gué-ri-son;
   mo-ments d'ac-ceuil, de com-mu-nion.

2. Jé-sus of-fre nos priè-res
   à ce Dieu plein de tendres-se.
   En ter-re sont les grains, nom-breux,
   sous les pluies d'un ciel gé-né-reux.

3. Pre-nons soin de cet-te ter-re
   que tou-jours Dieu re-nou-vel-le.
   Tou-te cré-a-tu-re de son chant
   loue-ra ce Dieu bon et clé-ment.

4. Ap-pro-chez-vous de la dan-se;
   ve-nez, chan-tez vos lou-an-ges.
   pour la jus-tice et pour la paix;
   Vie de Dieu sur le monde en-tier.

5. Ô Jé-sus à cet-te ta-ble,
   tu nous as fait une pla-ce,
   gran-de com-mu-nau-té d'a-mis,
   dans ton a-mour, dans ton Es-prit.

198 When We Gather at the Table

(Quand nous venons à la table)

Unison
♩ = 84

1 When we gath-er at the ta-ble wine is poured and
2 Je - sus of-fers our thanks-giv-ing bless-ing God for
3 Word of pro-mise claims at-ten-tion earth re-newed by
4 Come, in-vit-ed, now draw near-er, join this ho-ly
5 Christ, your com-ing and your host-ing gives us place at

bread is bro-ken. Then love claims us, of-fering
life we're giv-en. From the earth comes grain to
God's de-sig-ning. All the crea-tures join in
ce-le-bra-tion. Here be strength-ened, called to
wi-dening ta-ble now em-brac-ing world and

heal-ing, we hear wel-come, gent-ly spo-ken.
feed us wa-tered by the rains of hea-ven.
prais-es — God's in-ten-ded whole-ness find-ing.
jus-tice, liv-ing now God's new cre-a-tion.
neigh-bour Spi-rit strong, by love en-a-bled.

See previous page for French translation.

Words: Walter Farquharson, 1995; French translation: David Fines, 2006
Music: Ron Klusmeier, 2006
Words copyright © 1995 by Walter Farquharson. Used by permission.
Music copyright © 2006 by Ron Klusmeier, www.musiklus.com. Used by permission.
French translation copyright © 2006 David Fines. Used by permission.

When at This Table

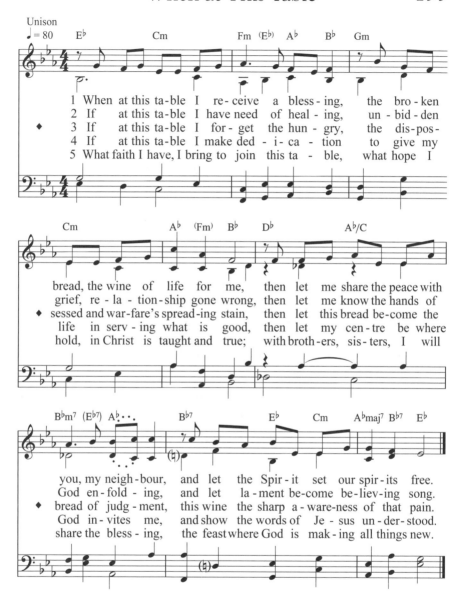

Unison
♩ = 80

1 When at this ta-ble I re-ceive a bless-ing, the bro-ken
2 If at this ta-ble I have need of heal-ing, un-bid-den
3 If at this ta-ble I for-get the hun-gry, the dis-pos-
4 If at this ta-ble I make ded-i-ca-tion to give my
5 What faith I have, I bring to join this ta - ble, what hope I

bread, the wine of life for me, then let me share the peace with
grief, re-la-tion-ship gone wrong, then let me know the hands of
sessed and war-fare's spread-ing stain, then let this bread be-come the
life in serv-ing what is good, then let my cen-tre be where
hold, in Christ is taught and true; with broth-ers, sis-ters, I will

you, my neigh-bour, and let the Spir-it set our spir-its free.
God en-fold-ing, and let la-ment be-come be-liev-ing song.
bread of judg-ment, this wine the sharp a-ware-ness of that pain.
God in-vites me, and show the words of Je-sus un-der-stood.
share the bless-ing, the feast where God is mak-ing all things new.

Words: Shirley Erena Murray, 2004
Music: Jane Marshall, 2005
Words copyright © 2004 and music copyright © 2006 Hope Publishing Company,
Carol Stream, IL 60188. All rights reserved. Used by permission.

FEASTDAY
11 10 11 10
Alternate tune: O PERFECT LOVE

200 You Are My Body

Unison
♩ = 72

1 "You are my bo - dy!" Joy and won - der! As - sem - bled
2 "This is my bo - dy!" Sim - ple Glo - ry! – a cup of
3 At one with Christ, a - round the ta - ble where all may
4 We are your bo - dy! One in Spir - it, dear Christ, with

in our Sav - iour's name, our scat - tered spir - its glad - ly
wine, a loaf of bread feed us, and join us to the
eat, and no - thing pay, where all are hon - oured and en -
all your church, we pray your bo - dy - lan - guage to in -

gath - er the Way of Je - sus to pro -
stor - y of Christ, a - ris - en from the
a - bled, and none are scorned or turned a -
her - it. Come, lead us in your truth - ful

claim. Come Spir - it, weave us in - to one, to
dead, whose Life, for - ev - er flow - ing free, en -
way, we pro - phe - sy, with brok - en bread, a
way! To seek for what is fair and right: shall

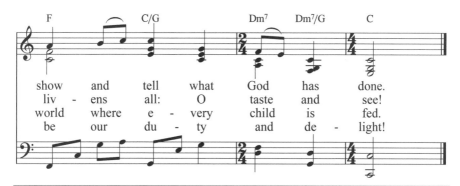

show and tell what God has done.
liv - ens all: O taste and see!
world where e - very child is fed.
be our du - ty and de - light!

Words: Brian Wren, 1993
Music: Judith Snowdon, 2006
Words copyright © 1996 Hope Publishing Company, Carol Stream, IL 60188. All rights reserved.
Used by permission.
Music copyright © Judith Snowdon 2006. Used by permission.

HAZEL
9 8 9 8 8 8
Alternate tune: NEUMARK

I Am the Bread of Life 201

I am the bread of life bro-ken for the world, I am the
cup poured out for all. Those who be-lieve in me will
nev - er die. I am the life of the world.

Words and music: Tom Kacemarek; arr. Paul A. Tate
Words and music copyright © 2005, World Library Publications, 3708 River Rd., Suite 400, Franklin Park, IL 60131-2158. 800-566-6150.
www.wlpmusic.com. All rights reserved. Used by permission.

202

Bread for the Journey
(Pain pour la route)

English: Bread for the jour - ney, food for the way.
French: *Pain pour la rou - te, pour nos che - mins.*

(for the jour -ney)
(pour la rou- te)

Cup of God's bles - sing, to -
De Dieu la cou - pe, au -

(food for the way)
(pour nos che -mins)

(God's bles - sing)
(la cou - pe)

mor - row, to - day.
jourd'- hui, de - main.

(to - mor - row, to - day)
(au - jourd'-hui, de - main)

Words and music: Bruce Harding, 2000; French trans. David Fines, 2005
Words and music copyright © 2000 by Bruce Harding, www.evensong.ca. Used by permission.
French translation copyright © 2005 by David Fines. Used by permission.

Kingsfold Communion Set
Holy, Holy, Holy (Sanctus and Benedictus)

203

O ho-ly, ho-ly ho-ly God, O God of time and space. All

earth and sea and sky a-bove bear wit-ness to your grace. Ho -

san-na in the high-est heav'n, cre - a - tion sings your praise. And

bles-sed is the One who comes and bears your name al - ways!

Memorial Acclamation

204

Sing Christ has died and Christ is ri - sen, Christ will come a - gain! Sing

Christ has died and Christ is ri - sen, Christ will come a - gain!

Great Amen

205

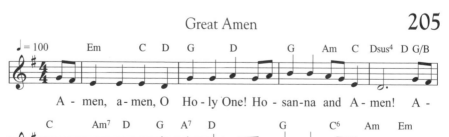

A - men, a - men, O Ho - ly One! Ho - san-na and A - men! A -

men, a - men, O Ho - ly One, Ho - san - na and A - men!

Words: William S. Kervin and Paul Stott
Music: traditional melody, England and Ireland
Words copyright © 2005 William S. Kervin and Paul Stott. Used by permission.

KINGSFOLD
8 6 8 6 D

Patriquin Communion Set

206 Holy, Holy, Holy (Sanctus and Benedictus)

Memorial Acclamation

Great Amen

A communion set excerpted from Patriquin's "A Caribbean Mass."

Words: traditional liturgical text
Music: Donald Patriquin, 1998
Music copyright © 1998/1999 Donald Patriquin, www.donaldpatriquin.com. A Tempo, PO Box 72, Eastman, QC J0E 1P0 Canada. Used by permission.

209 Go, Make a Diff'rence

Words and Music: Steve Angrisano and Tom Tomaszek, 1997
Copyright © 1997, Steve Angrisano and Tom Tomaszek. Published by spiritandsong.com ®. All rights reserved. Used with permission.

see   the love of   God   for you and me.   We are the
need,   the face of   God   for all to   see.   We are the

light   of the world,   not to be hid-den but   be   seen.
spir - it of hope;   we are the   voice of peace.

Go   make a diff - 'rence in the world.

D.C.

3 So   let your love shine   on,   let it shine for all   to   see.

Go   make a diff - 'rence in the   world.   And the

spir - it of Christ will be with us as we go.

Go make a diff - 'rence in the world.

D.C. al Fine

210 Jesus, Loving Lord
(Yeshu supriya)

Sanskrit: Ye - shu su - pri - ya,
English: Je - sus, lov - ing Lord;

Tabla or other hand drums

Dha Te Te Tin Tin Na Na Dhin Dhin Dha Te Te Tin Tin Na Na Dhin Dhin
X 0 X 0

Drums and drone continue throughout

Drone

This Christian bhajan or devotional song is meant to be sung in unison, accompanied by a drone and by drums, if available. Try playing the drone on organ, accordion, or other sustaining instruments, or invite people to sing it. The rhythm indicated is the rhythmic outline for Kehrva Taal, an eight-beat pattern traditionally used for devotional songs.

Words and music: traditional song, India; arr. *More Voices*, 2007
Rhythm arr. Amarjeet Singh Vabhana, 2006
Arrangement copyright © .
Rhythm arrangement copyright © 2006 Amarjeet Singh Vabhana. Used by permission.

Ye - shu a - shra - ye, Ye - shu pri - ya
Je - sus, strength and stay, in your mer - cy

ta - ra - ka, sa - ha - ya ho - ma - la.
bless us all and keep us night and day.

Go Now in Peace, Guided by the Light 211
(Vayan en paz)

Unison
♩ = 138

Spanish: Va - yan en paz, guia - dos por la luz del Se -
English: Go now in peace, guid - ed by the light of

ñor, a con - tem - plar
Christ, so you may be

la Pa - la - bra vi - va de Dios.
nour - ished by the Word of Life.

A commissioning and prayer for guidance.

Words and music: Pedro Rubalcava, 2002; arrangement: Peter Kolar, 2002
Words and music copyright © 2002, World Library Publications, 3708 River Rd., Suite 400, Franklin Park, IL 60131-2158. 800-566-6150. www.wlpmusic.com. All rights reserved. Used by permission.

212 Sent Out in Jesus' Name
(Enviado soy de Dios)

Spanish: En - via - do soy de Dios, mi ma - no lis-ta es-tá pa-ra cons-tru - ir con El un mun-do fra - ter - nal. Los án - ge-les no son en - via - dos a cam-biar un mun-do de do-lor por un mun-do de paz. Me ha to-ca-do a mí ha-cer-lo rea-li-dad; a - yú-da-me, Se-ñor, a ha - cer tu vo-lun - tad.

English: Sent out in Je-sus' name, our hands are rea-dy now to make the world the place in which the king-dom comes. The an - gels can-not change a world of hurt and pain in-to a world of love, of jus-tice and of peace. The task is ours to do, to set it real-ly free. O, help us to o-bey, and car-ry out your will.

Words and music: traditional song, Cuba
English trans. Jorge Maldonado; arr. More Voices, 2007
English translation copyright © 1988 ABINGDON PRESS (Administered by THE COPYRIGHT COMPANY NASHVILLE, TN).
All rights reserved. International Copyright Secured. Used by permission.
Arrangement copyright © .

Take Up His Song

Take up his song of peace* and go in-to the world. Take up his song of peace* in ev-'ry mo-ment.

In ev-'ry mo-ment of the jour-ney, we're lay-ing down our lives; lay them down, in peace,* lay them down, and take up his song.

* additional verses: "hope," "faith," and "love."

This song of commitment was written in response to Colin Gibson's hymn "He came singing love."

Words and music: Laura A. Herman, 2005; arr. Robin King, 2006
Words and music: copyright © 2005 Laura A. Herman, Box 81, Arcola, SK S0C 0G0. Used by permission.
Arrangement copyright © 2006 Robin King, Edmonton, AB. Used by permission.

214   May God's Sheltering Wings

May God's shel-ter-ing wings, her* gath-er-ing wings pro-
tect you. May God's nur-tur-ing arms, her*
crad-ling arms sus-tain you, and
hold you in her* love, and hold you in her* love.

* alternative: "his"

A blessing for baptism, for healing prayer, and for the close of worship.

Words and music: Judith Snowdon, 2004
Words and music copyright © 2004 by Judith Snowdon. Used by permission.

Peace Be with You

Actions for "Peace be with you":

Peace be with you: Extend one arm and hand forward in "peace sign."

Peace forever: Extend other arm and hand forward in "peace sign."

Peace be with you, my friend: Extend both arms and hands forward in "peace signs" then arms down, palms facing out.

Till we meet again, may God be with you: Hold hands, travelling or rocking in beat.

Peace, peace, peace: Extend one arm and hand in "peace sign" for first word, then change arms for second word, then both arms and hands out together for last "peace."

A blessing song with actions. The actions can be repeated with line/circle travelling in other direction.

Words and music: Alison L. Wesley (Slaats), 2000
Words and music copyright © Alison L. Wesley (Slaats). Used by permission.

216 Wherever You May Go

Wher - ev - er you may go, I will fol - low, and your peo - ple shall be my peo - ple too. Wher - ev - er you may go, I will fol - low, for I would be faith - ful, loy - al and true.

1 Say the word and I will stay, I will ne - ver go a - way,
2 From be - gin - ning to the end I will al - ways be your friend,

Words and music: David Kai, 1996
Words and music copyright © 1996 by David Kai
c/o Pickering Village United Church, 300 Church St. N., Ajax, ON L1T 2W7. Used by permission.

RENAUD
Irregular

we will tra-vel side by side, and God's love will
when you need me, I'll be there, you can trust my

be our guide.
faith - ful care.

Hey Ney Yana

217

Hey ney ya - na, hey ney ya - na,

hey ney ya - na, hey ya hey yo, hey ya hey yo.

1 I walk in beau - ty, yes I do, yes I do, I
2 I leave in beau - ty, yes I do, yes I do, I

talk in beau - ty, yes I do, yes I do, I
sleep in beau - ty, yes I do, yes I do, I

sing of beau - ty, hey ya hey yo, hey ya hey yo.
dream of beau - ty, hey ya hey yo, hey ya hey yo.

The syllables in the chorus of this song of respect for Creation are vocables, non-lexical syllables meant as vehicles for praise. Try this song unaccompanied or with a hand drum accenting the beginning of each measure.

Words and music: Brook Medicine Eagle, as taught by Leonard Eagle Cloud Howell
Words and music copyright © Brooke Medicine Eagle, PMB C401, One 2nd Ave. East, Polson, MT 59860. Used by permission.

218 May the Love of the Lord
(Wei yuan Shen di ai)

* **alternative:** "our God"

ci - ai ban - sui ni.
and be grac - ious to you.

Wu - lun he - chu
May God's Spir - it

ta di ling dou yong - yuan ban - sui ni.
be up - on you as you leave this place.

A simple improvisation of the accompaniment is encouraged for this blessing song.

Words: Maria Ling Poh Choo, Singapore
Music: Swee Hong Lim, Singapore
Words and music copyright © 2000 General Board of Global Ministries, GBGMusik, 475 Riverside Dr., New York, NY 10115. All rights reserved. Used by permission.

Ameni 219

♩ = 84

A - men - i, a - men - i,

Ba-ba - ba - ba - bam, ba-ba - ba - ba - bam,

a - men, a - men, a - men, a - men - i.

ba-ba-ba-ba - bam, ba-bam, ba- bam, ba-ba - ba - ba - bam.

"Ameni," pronounced Ah-meh-nee, is a South African variation of the word "Amen." Sing with any available combination of harmony parts, or make up your own.

Words: traditional liturgical text
Music: Composed by young men at Christ the New Man Parish, Ga-Rankuwa, South Africa, 1989
Transcribed and arranged by Dave Dargie
Transcription and arrangement copyright © Dave Dargie. Used by permission.

220 Hope Shines as the Solitary Star

This song can also be used as an Advent candle-lighting song by replacing the first word with "Peace," "Joy" and "Love" in subsequent weeks.

Words: Catherine Faith MacLean Music: Janet Bauman Tissandier
Words copyright © Catherine Faith MacLean.
Music copyright © Janet Bauman Tissandier, 2 – 825 - 7 St., Canmore, AB T1W 2C4. Used by permission.

221 I Am Walking a Path of Peace

lead me home. I am home.

* **additional verses:** "of love," "of grace," "of hope," "of joy," "with heart," etc.

Words and music: Janet Bauman Tissandier
Words and music copyright © Janet Bauman Tissandier, 2 – 825 - 7 St., Canmore, AB T1W 2C4. Used by permission.

May the Peace of God Be Your Peace   222

May the peace of God be your peace. May the love of God be the

love you show. May the joy of God be the joy you know, and

(be found in you.)
may the world that God would see be found in you.

This blessing is adapted for congregational use from a choral benediction.

Words and music: Neil McLaren, 2001, alt.
Words and music copyright © November 2001 Neil McLaren. nmclaren@rogers.com. Used by permission.

223
We Will Go with God
(Sizohamba Naye)

Xhosa: Si - zo-ham-ba na - ye! Ho, ho! ho! Si-zo-ham-ba na - ye!
English: We will go with God! Ho, ho, ho! We will go with God!

ye!   Ngo-mhla we-nja - bu-lo   si - zo-ha-mba na-
God!   On this day of great joy   we will go with

Ngo- mhla, ho!
This day, oh!

ye.   Ngo-mhla we-nja - bu-lo   si-zo ha-mba na - ye.
God.   On this day of great joy   we will go with God.

Ngo-mhla, ho!
This day, oh!

Xhosa pronunciation: *See-zoh-hahm-bah nah-yay... Goom-shla weh-njah-boo-loh... (the "shla" sound in "Goom-shla" should be an aspirated "h" sound rather than a full "sh" sound).*

Words and music: traditional song, Swaziland and South Africa; arr. Dave Dargie
Arrangement copyright © Dave Dargie. Used by permission.

224
May the God of Peace
(Na Jijoho)

Goun: Na Ji-jo-ho, ji - jo-ho ni tin. Na Ji-jo-ho,
English: May the God of peace and of all good, may the God of

ji - jo-ho ni tin. Po ome-po - po. A -
peace and of all good be al-ways with you. A -

men. Po ome-po - po. A - men!
men! May God's peace be with you. A - men!

A traditional blessing, **Goun pronunciation:** *Nah Jee-joh-hoh, jee-joh-hoh nee tihn. Poh ohm-poh-poh. Ah-mehn.*

Words and music: traditional song, Benin; English trans. S T Kimbrough, Jr.
Arrangement:
English translation copyright © 2004 General Board of Global Ministries, GBGMusik, 475 Riverside Dr., New York, NY 10115. Used by permission.
Arrangement copyright © .

Amen 225

A - men, a - men, a - men.

A - men, a - men, a - men.

A - men, a - men, a - men.

A - men, a - men, a - men.

Part 2 is the melodic retrograde of Part 1. Try Part 1 with your congregation, with the choir singing Part 2, or split into two groups and enjoy the harmony.

Words: traditional liturgical text
Music: traditional melody, China; arrangement: Puqi Jiang, China
Music arrangement copyright © Christian Conference of Asia. Used by permission.

Copyright Holders

Abramsky, David. www.davidabramsky.com

Asian Institute for Liturgy and Music.
PO Box 10533 Broadway Centrum, Quezon City
1141, Philippines. Ph:011-63-2-722-1490.
admin@ailm.net

Augsburg Fortress Press.
PO Box 1209, Minneapolis, MN 55440-1209.
www.augsburgfortress.org

Bauman, Lynn.
PRAXIS, 737 PR 249, Telephone, TX 75488.
praxis@netexas.net

Best, Jane. www.bestsongs.ca

Borealis Music. www.LinneaGood.com

Bumba, Edo. edobumbo@bredband.net

Burks, Leonard.
Legre Publishing Company, 1970 E 84th Street,
Cleveland, OH 44103-4225. Lgb3@prodigy.net

Camacho, Joe.
BILAC, PO Box 706, Volcano, HI 96785.
Kanoe35712@aol.com

Caribbean Conference of Churches.
PO Box 876, Port of Spain, Trinidad.
Fax: 1-868-662-1303.
trinidad-headoffice@ccc-caribe.org.
www.ccc-caribe.org

Choristers Guild.
2834 W. Kingsley Rd., Garland, TX 75041-2498.
Fax: 972-840-3113. www.choristersguild.org

Christian Conference of Asia.
PO Box 183 Chiang Mai, Amphur Muang,
Chiang Mai 50000 Thailand.
Fax: 011-66-53-247-303. cca@cca.org.hk

Common Cup Company. www.commoncup.com

Copyright Company, The.
1025 16th Avenue South, Nashville, TN 37212.
Fax: 615-321-1099. www.thecopyrightco.com

Dargie, Dave.
Melusinenstr. 13 D-81671 Muenchen, Germany.
Ph/Fax 011-49-89-49-16-92.

Desert Flower Music.
Box 1476, Carmichael, CA 95609.
www.strathdeemusic.com

Donaldson, Andrew.
14 Hambly Ave., Toronto, ON M4E 2R6.
seraph@pathcom.com

EMI Christian Music.
101 Winners Circle, Brentwood, TN 37027.
Fax: 615-371-6897. www.emicmg.com

Emmaus Productions. www.emmausproductions.com

Erhardt, Lori L.
Box 443, Oxbow, SK S0C 2B0.
bigdog.farm@sasktel.net

Farquharson, Walter.
Box 126, Saltcoats, SK S0A 3R0.
farq.blueheron@sasktel.net

Fines, David.
c/o The United Church of Canada, 3250 Bloor Street
West, Suite 300, Toronto, ON M8X 2Y4.
davidfines@egliseunie.org

Frayssé, Claude.
c/o Eglise Réformée de France, Allée de la grande
Musenne, 26750 Genissieux, France.
011-33-4-75-02-71-93

Gadeski, Janet.
c/o The United Church of Canada Foundation,
#300 – 3250 Bloor St. W., Toronto, ON M8X 2Y4.
jgadeski@united-church.ca

Gagnon, David-Roger.
2255, rue Chomedey, App. 16, Montréal, QC H3H
2B1. dgagnon@egliseunie.org

General Board of Global Ministries.
475 Riverside Drive, Room 350, New York, NY
10115. Fax: 212-870-3748. www.gbgm-umc.org

GIA Publications.
7404 S. Mason Avenue, Chicago, IL 60638.
www.giamusic.com

Gillette, Carolyn Winfrey.
Limestone Presbyterian Church, 3201 Limestone
Road, Wilmington, DE 19808-2198.
bcgillette@comcast.net

Graham, Fred.
c/o Emmanuel College, 75 Queen's Park Cres,
Toronto, ON M5S 1K7.

Graham, Melva Treffinger.
Grace Church on-the-hill, 300 Lonsdale Road,
Toronto, ON M4V 1X4. gracemusic2@rogers.com

Gunn, Rick.
Bedford United Church, 1200 Bedford Highway,
Bedford, NS B4A 1C3. info@rickgunn.com

Hann, David.
c/o Westmount-Leitches Creek Pastoral Charge,
15 MacLennan Drive, Westmount, NS B1R 1H6.
hann.david@ns.sympatico.ca

Hannah, Jim.
c/o Salmon Arm Pastoral Charge, PO Box 940,
Salmon Arm, BC V1E 4P1.

Harding, Bruce and Cheryl.
Evensong Worship Resources, www.evensong.ca

Herman, Laura A. Box 81, Arcola, SK S0C 0G0.

Hope Publishing Company.
380 S. Main Street, Carol Stream, IL 60188.
www.hopepublishing.com

ICEL Secretariat.
1522 K Street, NW, Suite 1000, Washington, DC
20005. permission@eliturgy.org

Kagawa Workshop.
Tokyaki Kagawa, 1025-1 Aza-Dohshiguchi
Asahisoshi Tsuru-shi, Yamanashi-ken,
Japan 402-0015.
Fax: 011-81-554-48-2486. kdw@kagawa-works.net

Kai, David.
c/o Pickering Village United Church, 300 Church
Street N., Ajax ON L1T 2W7.

Kervin, William S.
c/o Emmanuel College, 75 Queen's Park Cres,
Toronto, ON M5S 1K7.

King, Robin.
12028 - 140 Avenue, Edmonton, AB T5X 3T2.

Klusmeier, Ron.
Box 678, Parksville, BC V9P 2G7.
Fax: 250-954-1683. www.musiklus.com

Lankshear-Smith, Doreen.
PO Box 10155, Thunder Bay, ON P7B 6T7.

Lee, Stephen. Professional Music Services,
P.O. Box 791444, New Orleans, LA 70179-1444
pmsinc@bellsouth.net

L'Hirondelle, Cheryl. niya@ndnnrkey.net

MacLean, Catherine F.
12228 109 Ave., Edmonton, AB T5M 2E3.

Makumira University.
Rev. Dr. Gwakisa Mwakagali, PO Box 55, Usa
River, Tanzania. Fax: 011-255-27-255-3493.
provost@makumira.ac.tz

Maracle, Jonathan. www.brokenwalls.com

SOUTHMINSTER-STEINHAUER UNITED CHURCH

An Affirming Congregation within the United Church of Canada

Ministry Team: Nancy L. Steeves and Jim Spiers

Accompanist: Deb Mooney   March 21, 2010

WE GATHER AS SEEKERS

ED FOR THE SPIRIT:

If the only prayer you said in your whole life was "thank you"
that would suffice.   *Meister Eckhart*

ORDS OF WELCOME AND CANDLE LIGHTING

ATHERING SONG: *words and music Jim Strathdee*

The spirit in me greets the spirit in you, Alleluia.
God's in us and we're in God, Alleluia.

ORDS OF INVITATION: *Standing in body or spirit*

Response: … is reason enough for thanks.

NG: 154 MV, Deep in our Hearts

RAYER: *Together and seated*

irit of welcome, **for the bread of acceptance and the hospitality that**
eets us here, we **are** grateful. **For love and laughter, words and spaces,**
usic and silence, we give thanks. **For outstretched arms, for those who**
ait to hear how we are, for the presence that greets us in one another, we
are our delight. **May we offer welcoming love to one another as we**
are what we have with a hungry world, AMEN.

TO EXPLORE SACRED STORIES

EADING: A Child Helps Jesus   **(based on John 6:1-13)**
                    from The Family Story Bible by Ralph Milton
One: This is a story that has been passed down to us from the first century.
                    All: May we find wisdom for our living.

ONG: Tis a Gift to Be Simple

'Tis **a gift to be simple, 'tis a gift to be free,**
'Tis **a gift to come down where we ought to be,**
And when we find ourselves in the place just right,
T'will be in the valley of love and delight.
When true simplicity is gained,
to bow and to bend we shan't be ashamed.
To turn, turn will be our delight,
'till by turning, turning, we come 'round right.

SHARING STONE SOUP! A Cantata
Based on the musical by Linnea good and Scott Douglas
Originally directed by Greg Armstrong-Morris
Offered by the Adult Choir, Instrumental Ensemble and Friends
Directed by Deb Mooney

TO LIVE WITH DEEPER INTENTION

SONG: Turning of the World   *Words and Music by Ruth Pelham*

Let us sing this song for the turning_of the world.
That we may turn as one.
With ev'ry voice, with ev'ry song,
We will move this world along
And our lives will feel the echo of our turning.

With ev'ry voice! With ev'ry song!
We will move this world along.
With ev'ry voice, with ev'ry song,
We will move this world along
And our lives will feel the echo of our turning.

2. turning of our hearts,
3. turning of our hands

SHARING OUR LIFE AND WORK

SHARING OUR GIFTS

OFFERING OUR PRAYER:
Holy Mystery of all being: for food in a world where many walk in
hunger; for faith in a world where many walk in fear; for friends in a
world where many walk alone; we know and name our privilege. May
our thanksgiving become thanks-living, in the name of love, AMEN.

SHARING A SONG: 173 MV, Put Peace into Each Other's Hands

BLESSING

SONG FOR GOING: 156 MV, Dance with the Spirit
                                    Words and Music by Jim Stathdee

Dance with the spirit early in the mornin'
Walk with the spirit throughout the long day.
Work and hope for the new life a-bornin'
Listen to the spirit to show you the way.

SHARING STONE SOUP SOUTHMINSTER-STEINHAUER STYLE!

Essentials of Life

With eagerness and hope, these girls gather water in whatever containers they find.

In Canada, we cringe at the amount of plastic clogging landfill sites. However, in some places, a plastic container can catch an essential, life-giving substance: clean water from a communal well.

These girls from El Salvador represent the thousands of individuals we support through our grants to partners in many parts of the world. Our partners need assistance for basic needs such as agricultural programs and clean water. They also seek justice for Indigenous people confronting industrial development in their homeland. They long to know that people in other parts of the world care about their struggles. A common affirmation from our partners is, "Thank you for your support for our work among our people," quickly followed by a sincere entreaty: "Please continue to pray for us."

The Proverbs reading for today reminds us that wisdom was present from the beginning of the world, even from the start of every human life. May we be wise enough to know that God calls us to reach out in love through the **Mission and Service Fund** to assist people of every age, in Canada and around the world, to live in peace, hope, and justice.

The **Mission and Service Fund** transforms the lives of people in many parts of the world through the efforts of our global ecumenical partners. Your financial support and your prayer support do make a difference.

MISSION AND SERVICE FUND

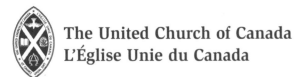

The United Church of Canada
L'Église Unie du Canada

Photo: Mary Fee (Photo location: San Rafael, El Salvador)   **Text:** Bill Steadman

Stone Soup!

The Cantata

based on the musical by

Scott Douglas & Linnea Good

Once upon a time two tricksters, Canny and Small, arrive in the tiny village named Oxter (Two Wandering Wonderers). They ask for a bite of supper, but the villagers refuse, so Canny and Small come up with a tricky plan, pretending to make "stone soup" with a magical soupstone (Stone Soup). The villagers are curious and end up adding ingredients from their own pockets in return for a taste of the magical soup. Everyone is so pleased with the soup that the mayor proposes a toast (S*O*U*P) and they all sing (Thanks To You). The villagers decide to pool their money and buy the stone from Canny and Small (We Need That Stone). The two tricksters accept the offer and hightail it out of town with the money. When the villagers next try to make soup, they realize they've been tricked. They chase after Canny and Small (Get Them! Instrumental) and drag them back to town (Get Them! Reprise). Luckily Small convinces the angry villagers that the magic of the soupstone lay in its having brought them together as a community (It Was You). All is forgiven, the tricksters are elected mayor and everyone celebrates (Stone Soup reprise).

Stone Soup Cast

Narrator:	Bill Robertson
Canny:	Shannon Mooney
Small:	Amber Rosborough
Mayor Rudy:	John Evans
Margaret:	Bernie Hardin
Villagers:	Trudy Smith
	Dorothy Swanson
	Sandi Lockhart
	Janet Dougan
	Allandra Power
	Bonnie Berg
	Mieke Wharton
	Pat Seale
	Blair Croft
	Bob Hetherington
	Carl McNamara
	Don Sheppard
	Ed Berg
	Jim Spears
	Lorne Lea
	Charles Bidwell
	Bill Hibbard
Musicians:	Pam Patten
	Rob McCracken
	Kathryne Kuhn
	April Cromack
Sound Technician:	Brayden Power

Marshall, Jane.
4077 Northaven Road, Dallas, TX 75229.
JAMM24@aol.com

Mayberry, Pat.
966 Sheridan Ave, Ottawa, ON K1Z 6M5.
www.patmayberry.com

McDade, Carolyn.
25 Woodridge Road, Orleans, PA 02653-4806.
surtsey@gis.net

Mclaren, Neil.
9 Woodland Glen Drive, Guelph, ON N1G 3N2.
nmclaren@rogers.com

Medicine Eagle, Brooke.
Singing Eagle Communications, PMB C401,
One 2nd Avenue East, Polson, MT 59806.
www.medicineeagle.com

Melhorn-Boe, David.
238 First Ave. E., North Bay, ON P1B 1J8.
mboe@ontera.net

Motum, Margaret.
470 Wickham St., Oshawa, ON L1K 1R9.

Mulrain, George.
c/o Methodist Conference Centre,
Belmont, PO Box 9, St John's, Antigua,
geomacdmul@yahoo.com

Music Services Org.
Vineyard Songs. 209 Chapelwood Drive,
Franklin, TN 37069. 615-794-9015.
info@musicservices.org

Mxadana, Gobingca George.
Imilonji kaNtu Choral Society,
6942 Malie Street, PO Orlando
SOWETO 1804, Johannesburg, Republic of
South Africa. www.imilonji.co.za

Naytowhow, Joseph.
c/o Cheryl L'Hirondelle, niya@ndnnrkey.net

Nixon, Bryn.
12 – 10820 Springmont Drive, Richmond, BC V7E 3S5.
bryn.nixon@telus.net

Odney, Blair. bodney@uniserv.com

O'Driscoll, Herbert.
1000 Jasmine Avenue, Victoria, BC V8Z 2P4.

Ohtomo, Estate of Frank Y.
c/o Mrs. Naoko Okumichi-Eisele,
Koenigsteiner Str. 48,
65812 Bad Soden / Ts, Germany.
Ph/fax: 011-49-6196-63611.

Oldham, John.
76 Marygrove Crescent, Winnipeg, MB R3Y 1M2.
204-489-6919. johnomar@mts.net

Oregon Catholic Press.
PO Box 18030, Portland, OR 97218-0030.
www.ocp.org

Patriquin, Donald.
CP 72, Eastman, QC J0E 1P0.
www.donaldpatriquin.com

Pattison, Julian. www.eaglewingmusic.org

Pedersen, Lydia.
102 Burnhamthorpe Road, Toronto, ON M9A 1H2.

Petricko, William. willpetricko@hotmail.com

Pilgrim Press.
700 Prospect Avenue, Cleveland, OH 44115-1100.
www.thepilgrimpress.com

Rice, Delbert.
3705 Nueva Vizcaya, Imugan, Santa Fe, Philippines.

Robertson, Alison M.
3 Ross Gardens, Edinburgh, EH9 3BS, Scotland.

Robertson, David.
c/o High River United Church, PO Box 5520, High
River, AB T1V 1M4.

Rumbolt, Paul. www.paulrumbolt.com

Selah Publishing.
PO Box 98066, Pittsburgh, PA 15227.
Fax: 412-886-1022. www.selahpub.com

Signpost Music. www.signpostmusic.com

Singh, Amarjeet. amarrhythm@hotmail.com

Singh, Harkanwal. Dilruba_beloved@hotmail.com

Skibsted, Rev. Louise. iskib9@telus.net

Slaats, Alison L.
196 Broad Leaf Crescent, Ancaster, ON L9G 3N1.
www.alisonslaats.com

Smith, Elizabeth J.
624 Centre Road, Bentleigh, VIC 3165, AUS.
ejsmith@pacific.net.au

Snowdon, Judith.
1055 Saint Joseph Road, Saint Joseph-de-Kent,
NB E3S 4C7.

Sosa, Pablo.
Espartaco 634, 1406 Buenos Aires, Argentina.
Fax: 011-54-11-4633-2825. sosasilva@infovia.com.ar

Souledre, Denise.
5 – 206 Candlewood Cres., Waterloo, ON N2L 5Y9.
moresoul@rogers.com

Spencer, Stephen.
38 Goldsboro Ave., Riverview NB E1B 4K4.

Stilborn, Elizabeth A.
#217 – 330 Plainsview Drive, Regina, SK S4S 6Z8.
elizabeth.stilborn@uregina.ca

Stott, Paul.
754 Manning Avenue, Toronto, ON M6G 2W4.

Stubbington, Marg. Glebe St. James United Church,
650 Lyon Street South, Ottawa, ON K1S 3Z7.
music650.glebestjames@bellnet.ca

Svenson, Paul B.
Dad's Songbook Music, 12463 Rancho Bernardo Rd.,
#123, San Diego, CA 92128. www.dadsongbook.com

Tice, Adam M. L.
911 N. 6th Street, Goshen, IN 46528. amltice@yahoo.com

Tissandier, Janet Bauman.
2 – 825 7th St., Canmore, AB T1W 2C4.

TKO Licensing Limited/Whole Armour Publishing.
PO Box 130, Hove, East Sussex, BN3 6QU UK.
www.tkogroup.com

Tufts, S. Curtis.
178 Greenwood Drive, Spruce Grove, AB T7X 1Y7.

Watson Henderson, Ruth.
r_watson-henderson@hotmail.com

Wayne Leupold Editions.
8510 Triad Drive, Colfax, NC 27235.

Wehlander, Keri K. www.creativeworship.ca

Weisensel, Neil. www.neilmusic.com

Whitmore, Alan.
5 – 206 Candlewood Cres., Waterloo, ON N2L 5Y9.
moresoul@rogers.com

Wilcox, Diana. dlcwilcox@shaw.ca

Willow Publishing Pty Ltd.
PO Box 288, Brookvale NSW 2100, Australia.
www.willowconnection.com.au

Woolfrey, Sid. 4 Coozes Road, Hillgrade, NL A0G 2S0.

World Council of Churches Publications Office.
150, Route de Ferney, PO Box 2100, 1211 Geneva 2,
Switzerland. Fax: 011-41-22-798-1346.

World Library Publications.
Box 2701, Schiller Park, IL 60176.
www.wlpmusic.com.

Wright, Patricia. patriciaw@metunited.org

Sources for Hymns and Songs

Abramsky, David 149
African-American spiritual 88, 167
Alonso, Tony...28
Angrisano, Steve......................................109, 209
Aymer, Birchfield..13
Bach, Johann Sebastian......................................73
Badejo, Emmanuel...59
Balchin, Ivy... 5
Barnhart, Leslie Palmer 63
Batastini, Robert 43
Bauman, Lynn 95, 96, 123
Bell, John 2, 42, 57, 67, 77, 85, 89, 90, 110,
....112, 115, 166, 193, 196
Bell, Steve...119
Berthier, Jacques 16, 75, 83, 86, 100
Best, Jane 155, 159
Bittner, Mary..93, 172
Bloss, Michael...145
Brennan, Dan...46
Bringle, Mary Louise 43, 159
Brown, Monica 15
Brown, Brenton...4, 26
Bumba, Edo...104
Burks, Leonard...185
Camacho, Joe 103
Canedo, Ken...6, 46, 113
Caribbean Conference of Churches 124, 192
Cavallero, Marc..46
Chepponis, James.. 11
Choo, Maria Ling Poh..218
Clyde, Arthur..79
Composer unknown 37, 169
Cooney, Rory 120, 128
Damon, Dan ..38, 40, 44, 81, 94, 101, 133, 137, 139,
....161, 176, 177, 186
Dargie, David...219, 223
Daw, Jr., Carl...20, 49, 80
de Hall, Sara M. 76
Doerksen, Brian 26
Donaldson, Andrew.....................12, 138, 163, 187
Duck, Ruth ... 10, 30, 65, 71, 72, 74, 79, 126, 143, 148
Duncan, Norah 50
English Hymnal 111
Erhardt, Lori...147
Farquharson, Walter 35, 198
Farrell, Bernadette...114
Fedak, Alfred V. 20
Fines, David 1, 3, 7, 21, 23, 36, 58, 62,
.........................67, 68, 69, 70, 85, 90, 91, 96,
.... 104, 122, 135, 161, 176, 187, 193, 202
Fraysse, Claude...57
Gadeski, Janet 134
Gagnon, David-Roger..................67, 91, 108, 197
Gelineau, Joseph 170
Gibson, Colin 17
Gillette, Carolyn Winfrey.........................111, 136
Gondo, Alexander 2
Good, Linnea....8, 31, 37, 84, 92, 95, 96, 121, 123, 130
Graham, Fred 24, 93
Graham, Melva Treffinger 169
Gunn, Rick 106, 171, 194

Habel, Norman...................................39, 55, 152
Hann, David 7
Hannah, Jim 87, 174, 180
Harding, Bruce....14, 47, 62, 91, 122, 136, 144, 147,
...................................150, 157, 162, 183, 202
Harding, Cheryl...157
Hart, Sarah 182
Hassler, Hans Leo..73
Haugen, Marty 1, 73, 143
Henderson, Ruth Watson.............................65, 190
Herman, Laura...213
Hong, Lim Swee 218
Husberg, Amanda..64
Im, Song-suk 129
International Commission
    on English in the Liturgy, The...................25, 109
Jiang, Pugi 225
Kaan, Fred..22, 23, 173
Kabemba, Joseph 140
Kacemerek, Tom 201
Kagawa, Toyohiko 125
Kai, David 216
Kasbohm, Donna...10
Kervin, William S. 69, 203, 204, 205
Kimbrough, Jr., S.T. 34, 58, 107, 168, 224
King, Robin...213
Klusmeier, Ron 23, 30, 35, 82, 98, 154, 158, 173,
....178, 198
Kolar, Peter 211
Lankshear-Smith, Doreen 149
Lee, Song-chon 129
Lee, Stephen...88, 167
L'Hirondelle, Cheryl 141
Light, Gordon..............................12, 138, 145, 163
Loh, I-to 2, 22, 184, 187
Macdonald, Ian 163
MacLean, Catherine...220
Mahler, Michael 72
Maldonado, Jorge..212
Manibusan, Jesse...25
Maracle, Jonathan 160
Marshall, Jane 199
Matsikenyiri, Patrick..............................38, 189
Maule, Graham 85, 90
May, Janet W...76
Mayberry, Pat......................48, 127, 135, 195
McCarthy, Michele 191
McDade, Carolyn...............................41, 165
McLaren, Neil 222
Medicine Eagle, Brooke.....................................217
Melhorn-Boe, David........................87, 174, 180
Michaels, Patrick...80
Monteiro, Simei 54, 108
More Voices 19, 33, 36, 38, 45, 52, 58, 59, 66, 68,
...................97, 99, 107, 131, 188, 210, 212, 224
Morris, Sally Ann 74
Motum, Margaret 153
Mulrain, George.....................................116, 131
Murray, Shirley Erena........28, 64, 78, 158, 178, 199
Mxadana, George 151
Naytowhow, Joseph 141

Nixon, Bryn..69, 142
Nkuinji, Abel...34
Nsakazongwe, Daisy...............................187
Odney, Blair...136
O'Driscoll, Herbert...................................53
Ohtomo, Frank Y...125
Olangi, Paul-Jean..151
Oldham, John....................82, 98, 147, 154
Oliano, Ramon & Sario.............................181
Olson, Howard S...97
Patriquin, Donald.....................206, 207, 208
Pattison, Julian...3, 32
Pedersen, Lydia.....................41, 165, 190
Pegura, Federico...193
Petricko, Will..175
Prescod, Patrick...............13, 118, 124, 192
Redman, Matt...29
Reindorf, Dinah...70
Rice, Delbert...181
Robertson, Alison..89
Robertson, David...61
Robertson, Glenn..4
Roth, Kevin..46
Rowan, William..126
Rubalcava, Pedro.......................................211
Rumbolt, Paul.......................................51, 191
Schalk, Carl F..49
Scruggs, Randy...18
Shangjuan, Grace..5
Shwe, Saw Gideon Tun................................56
Sikh traditional text....................................105
Singh Sahota, Harkanwal...........................105
Singh Vabhana, Amarjeet...................105, 210
Skibsted, Louise..19
Slaats, Alison...215
Smith, Elizabeth..17
Snowdon, Judith.............27, 53, 148, 179, 200, 214
Sosa, Pablo..68, 76
Soulodre, Denise.....................................88, 145
Spencer, Stephen..194
Stilborn, Elizabeth.............................117, 132
Stott, Paul...............................203, 204, 205
Strathdee, Jim..........................21, 78, 156
Stubbington, Marg..........48, 127, 135, 195
Sutton, Joan..108
Svenson, Paul..142
Taizé Community...............9, 16, 75, 86, 100,
....102, 146, 164, 170
Tai, Nai-chen...60
Takahashi, Ushio..125

Tan, Timothy..60
Tate, Paul...201
Taylor, Godfrey..116
Thompson, John W..18
Tice, Adam..24
Tissandier, Janet...............................220, 221
Tomaszek, Tom..............................182, 209
traditional Arabic..168
traditional Argentina..................................193
traditional Benin...224
traditional Cameroon.............................33, 99
traditional Caribbean..............................13, 116
traditional China...225
traditional Congo..104
traditional Cuba...212
traditional East Africa................................188
traditional Filipino.............................181, 184
traditional India..210
traditional Ireland..............................79, 120
traditional Ireland and England......203, 204, 205
traditional Jamaica.....................................118
traditional Latin America.............................58
traditional Lebanon.....................................168
traditional liturgical text.........19, 32, 36, 50, 52, 54,
..................................67, 68, 69, 70, 77, 83, 124,
..................................170, 206, 219, 225
traditional Mozambique................................38
traditional Nigeria (Yoruba).........................59
traditional Papua New Guinea......................22
traditional Peru..36
traditional South Africa..............45, 66, 151, 219
traditional Swaziland..................................223
traditional Tanzania......................................97
traditional Togo and Ghana........................107
traditional Uruguay.......................................52
traditional Wales..111
True, Lori..71
Tufts, Curtis.......................................106, 162
University Christian Fellowship, Myanmar....56
Wang, Wei-fan..5
Warner, Steven....................................63, 171
Wehlander,Keri.................37, 84, 92, 169
Weisensel, Neil.................39, 51, 55, 152
Whitmore, Alan..191
Wilcox, Diana.....................................117, 132
Wong, W.H...5
Woolfrey, Sid...162
Wren, Brian.......................155, 176, 186, 200
Wright, Patricia...134
Zhong, Guo-ren...5

Scriptural References

GENESIS
Gen 1:2 39
Gen 1:3-5 103
Gen 1:10 41
Gen 1:11-12 135
Gen 1:26-27 44
Gen 1:27 27
Gen 1:31 190
Gen 2:5-6 55
Gen 2:7 ....27, 103, 150
Gen 5:22-24 223
Gen 6:9 223
Gen 7:36 106
Gen 8:22 135
Gen 9:6 44
Gen 11:6 141
Gen 14:18 198
Gen 18:9-15 190
Gen 21:1-7 190
Gen 27:28 55
Gen 28 172
Gen 32:30 27
Gen 37:8 74
Gen 41:8 74

EXODUS
Exod 3:2 98
Exod 3:5 ....42, 174
Exod 13:21 98
Exod 14:13 99
Exod 19:5 103
Exod 19:9 19
Exod 25:20 214
Exod 34:6 218
Exod 34:28 118

LEVITICUS
Lev 26:6 168

NUMBERS
Num 6:24-26 ....86, 218
Num 12:6 74
Num 31:23 5

DEUTERONOMY
Deut 6:5 79
Deut 7:6 11
Deut 7:9 103
Deut 8:3 196
Deut 14:2 11
Deut 28:6 12
Deut 30:9 174
Deut 30:16 89
Deut 31:6 109

RUTH
Ruth 1:16 216
Ruth 2:14 198

1 SAMUEL
1 Sam 2:1-9 120

1 Sam 3:4 ....161, 167
1 Sam 3:7-10 97
1 Sam 20:1 66

2 SAMUEL
2 Sam 24:17 66

1 KINGS
1 Kings 19:8 118
1 Kings 19:12 84

1 CHRONICLES
1 Chron 16:34 16
1 Chron 16:35 187
1 Chron 21:8 66
1 Chron 22:19 18
1 Chron 29:13 187

ESTHER
Esther 4:14 179

JOB
Job 7:13-14 74
Job 10:12 182
Job 33:4 ....135, 182
Job 38:7 190
Job 38:8-9 39

PSALMS
Psalm 1:3 117
Psalm 4:8 103
Psalm 5:11 ....40, 147
Psalm 6:9 175
Psalm 9:1-2 57
Psalm 10 ....72, 78
Psalm 15 18
Psalm 16:7 123
Psalm 16:11 81
Psalm 17:8 214
Psalm 18 17
Psalm 18:2 92
Psalm 18:3 51
Psalm 18:28 103
Psalm 19 31
Psalm 22 73
Psalm 23 60
Psalm 23:4 105
Psalm 23:5 94
Psalm 24:6 27
Psalm 27:4 217
Psalm 27:10 109
Psalm 27:14 175
Psalm 28:7 ....81, 150
Psalm 29:11 86
Psalm 30:1-11 156
Psalm 30:12 187
Psalm 31:2-3 92
Psalm 31:15 83
Psalm 32:1 95
Psalm 33:12 11
Psalm 34:8 104

Psalm 34:18 94
Psalm 36:7 214
Psalm 42 116
Psalm 42:2 27
Psalm 42:7 4
Psalm 43:3 ....31, 71
Psalm 46:1 84
Psalm 46:4 ....98, 163
Psalm 46:9 120
Psalm 46:10 77
Psalm 47:1 59
Psalm 48:1 51
Psalm 51:4 66
Psalm 51:10 15
Psalm 59:16-17 147
Psalm 63 109
Psalm 63:4 176
Psalm 65:9 ....144, 163
Psalm 66:4 61
Psalm 66:6 163
Psalm 66:19 175
Psalm 68:6 221
Psalm 68:9 144
Psalm 71:3 92
Psalm 74:21 179
Psalm 75:1 187
Psalm 78:52 106
Psalm 80:3, 7, 19 27
Psalm 80:5 143
Psalm 82:2-11 29
Psalm 84:8-10 119
Psalm 84:11 92
Psalm 85:8 222
Psalm 85:10 ....1, 24, 111, 173
Psalm 86:12 187
Psalm 86:15 218
Psalm 87:7 156
Psalm 89:1 147
Psalm 90:16 13
Psalm 91:1-2, 4 62
Psalm 91:4 214
Psalm 91:4-6 109
Psalm 91:15 96
Psalm 94:22 92
Psalm 95:1 ....9, 92
Psalm 95:5 181
Psalm 95:6 2
Psalm 96:1 180
Psalm 96:4 51
Psalm 97:6 182
Psalm 98:1 11
Psalm 98:4 61
Psalm 98:7 144
Psalm 103:1 176
Psalm 103:1-6 46
Psalm 103:6 45
Psalm 104 25
Psalm 104:1 130
Psalm 104:14-15 198
Psalm 104:24 55

Psalm 104:25-26 144
Psalm 104:29.......................... 103
Psalm 104:30........................... 15
Psalm 105:41........................ 144
Psalm 106:1............................. 16
Psalm 106:6........................... 66
Psalm 106:47........................ 187
Psalm 106:47-48 7
Psalm 107:1............................. 16
Psalm 107:22........................... 59
Psalm 113 60
Psalm 113:3............................. 51
Psalm 118........................22, 42
Psalm 118:1............................. 16
Psalm 118:19............................ 8
Psalm 118:24........................ 122
Psalm 118:28........................ 187
Psalm 118:29.......................... 16
Psalm 119:7........................ 196
Psalm 119:76........................ 165
Psalm 119:105........................ 108
Psalm 119:165.......................... 24
Psalm 121:1-2 129
Psalm 130:6......................... 143
Psalm 136..............................9
Psalm 136:16........................ 106
Psalm 138:1............................. 61
Psalm 139............................ 131
Psalm 139:7......................... 155
Psalm 139:11-12 103
Psalm 141............................. 73
Psalm 145:1-21 176
Psalm 145:3............................ 51
Psalm 147............................. 37
Psalm 147:3................94, 171
Psalm 147:8-18 181
Psalm 148............................ 30
Psalm 148:7-10 39
Psalm 149:3......................... 156
Psalm 150:4........................ 156

PROVERBS
Prov 3:2.............................. 143
Prov 3:17................................ 82
Prov 3:17-18............................ 63
Prov 4:18...................... 108, 220
Prov 8:1-36 10
Prov 8:22-31....................... 145
Prov 8:34............................. 63
Prov 9:5.............................. 198
Prov 12:28.......................... 221
Prov 22:9........................... 173
Prov 31:20......................... 136

ECCLESIASTES
Eccl 3:1-8 ....24, 136, 165
Eccl 3:4 156
Eccl 3:19 103
Eccl 5:3-7 74
Eccl 12:9 126

SONG OF SONGS
Song of Songs 5:2 94
Song of Songs 7:8-9................. 63
Song of Songs 8:6 .... 85, 135

ISAIAH
Isa 6:3.....................41, 203, 206
Isa 9:6............................ 111, 224
Isa 10:1-4 78
Isa 11:2 6
Isa 12:2.............................. 109
Isa 12:3.............................. 222
Isa 25:8 120
Isa 28:5 217
Isa 29:8 74
Isa 29:23............................ 179
Isa 30:26............................ 171
Isa 30:29................................ 81
Isa 32:17............................ 143
Isa 35:6-7 144
Isa 40:1 97
Isa 40:31............................ 175
Isa 41:9................................ 41
Isa 41:10 .... 105, 109, 119
Isa 42:5 135
Isa 42:10............................ 180
Isa 43:1 .... 161, 167
Isa 43:10 11
Isa 44:3.............................. 144
Isa 45:3-4 .... 161, 167
Isa 46:3-4 39
Isa 48:18............................ 144
Isa 54:10................................ 24
Isa 55:10-11........................ 135
Isa 55:12............................ 168
Isa 57:19............................ 149
Isa 58:6-8 193
Isa 58:7 173
Isa 61:1............................. 45
Isa 61:1-3 97
Isa 62:3.............................. 217
Isa 66:1.................................. 1
Isa 66:13............................ 126

JEREMIAH
Jer 30:17............................ 171
Jer 31:4-13 156
Jer 31:9............................. 221
Jer 33:9............................. 171
Jer 33:10-11...................... 16, 147
Jer 33:11............................ 222
Jer 34:15............................ 182

LAMENTATIONS
Lam 3:22-23............................ 28
Lam 3:25-26 175

EZEKIEL
Ezek 1:4 55
Ezek 1:23-25 214

Ezek 11:19........................ 44, 154
Ezek 20:10 106
Ezek 46:12 5
Ezek 47:1-12 144
Ezek 47:5-12 163
Ezek 47:12.......................... 135

DANIEL
Dan 2:1-2 74
Dan 2:23............................ 187
Dan 2:28............................... 74
Dan 3 43
Dan 3:16............................ 139
Dan 5:11-14 6
Dan 9:4-5 66

HOSEA
Hos 2:19-20......................... 100
Hos 6:3 144
Hos 11:12 223

JOEL
Joel 2:26............................ 179
Joel 2:28 .... 74, 84

AMOS
Amos 2:10............................ 106
Amos 5:8.............................. 41
Amos 5:24............................ 117

MICAH
Mic 4:3 120
Mic 6:8 .... 89, 223
Mic 7:7 175

NAHUM
Nah 1:3.................................. 55

ZECHARIAH
Zech 9:10 148
Zech 10:1 55
Zech 8:19 13

MALACHI
Mal 3:1 11

WISDOM
Wisdom 7:22-30........................ 10

SIRACH
Sirach 51:13-22 63

MATTHEW
Matt 1:23....................... 47, 166
Matt 2:13-23........................ 111
Matt 3:11 155
Matt 3:16.............................. 3
Matt 4:1 106
Matt 4:4 196
Matt 4:1-11........................ 118
Matt 4:18-22....................... 113

Matt 5:3-11 205
Matt 5:6 109
Matt 5:8 12
Matt 5:13-16 .... 80, 209
Matt 5:23-24 76
Matt 5:38-42 94
Matt 6:10 151
Matt 6:26 126
Matt 7:7-8 94
Matt 7:9 65
Matt 7:24-25 92
Matt 8:23-27 153
Matt 9:18-26 .... 132, 186
Matt 9:20-22 161
Matt 9:21 89
Matt 10:1-8 212
Matt 10:13 222
Matt 10:17-21 113
Matt 11:28-30 97
Matt 12:18 182
Matt 12:46-50 178
Matt 13:33 155
Matt 14:23 133
Matt 14:29 138
Matt 16:24-26 113
Matt 17:20 174
Matt 18:20 14
Matt 19:13-15 133
Matt 19:16-26 113
Matt 20:1-16 127
Matt 21:1-9 128
Matt 23:34-40 162
Matt 23:37 214
Matt 24:42 19
Matt 25:31-46 .... 111, 114, 152
Matt 25:34 .... 12, 194
Matt 26:26-28 201
Matt 26:42 151
Matt 28:1 121
Matt 28:18-20 212
Matt 28:19-20 172

MARK
Mark 1:10 3
Mark 1:12-13 118
Mark 1:15 140
Mark 1:16-20 113
Mark 3:31-35 178
Mark 3:35 105
Mark 4:3-20 181
Mark 4:35-41 153
Mark 5:21-43 .... 132, 186
Mark 5:25-34 161
Mark 5:34 149
Mark 5:41-42 133
Mark 6:7 212
Mark 6:46 133
Mark 8:34-36 113
Mark 9:1 140
Mark 9:50 209

Mark 10:13-16 133
Mark 11:1-10 128
Mark 12:41-44 127
Mark 14:22-24 201
Mark 16:2 121
Mark 16:3 138

LUKE
Luke 1:13 175
Luke 1:17 6
Luke 1:26-38 11
Luke 1:35 75
Luke 1:46-55 .... 45, 120, 134
Luke 1:78-79 86
Luke 2:14 .... 36, 58, 124, 148
Luke 2:35 5
Luke 3:16 155
Luke 4:1 .... 3, 106
Luke 4:1-11 65
Luke 4:1-13 118
Luke 4:18 .... 45, 127
Luke 4:28 177
Luke 6:20-26 205
Luke 6:24-26 78
Luke 6:29 196
Luke 7:22 127
Luke 7:46-47 5
Luke 8:19-21 178
Luke 8:22-25 153
Luke 8:38-39 212
Luke 8:40 137
Luke 8:40-56 .... 132, 186
Luke 8:43-48 161
Luke 8:54-55 133
Luke 9:23-25 113
Luke 10:9 140
Luke 10:25-28 89
Luke 11:20 140
Luke 12:11 139
Luke 12:36 175
Luke 12:37 .... 19, 194
Luke 13:21 155
Luke 13:29 140
Luke 13:34 214
Luke 15:11-32 20
Luke 17:6 174
Luke 18:15-17 133
Luke 18:18-22 113
Luke 19:1-10 127
Luke 19:28-38 128
Luke 19:38 58
Luke 21:1-4 127
Luke 21:14-15 139
Luke 22:19-20 201
Luke 24:1, 22 121
Luke 24:30 199
Luke 24:32 21
Luke 24:36 .... 168, 215
Luke 24:32 79

JOHN
John 1:5 103
John 1:9 .... 31, 71
John 1:11-14 64
John 1:14 49
John 2:1-11 138
John 3:8 5
John 3:16 .... 100, 201
John 3:21 31
John 4:1-42 117
John 4:4-26 87
John 4:13-14 109
John 4:14 102
John 4:14-15 197
John 4:25 152
John 5:24 162
John 6:5-14 133
John 6:33-35, 48-51 ...... 194, 197
John 6:35 201
John 6:51 192
John 7:37 4
John 7:38 87
John 8:12 71
John 9:5 71
John 10:3 167
John 10:3 161
John 10:10 143
John 10:11-14 126
John 11 93
John 12:24 125
John 12:46 71
John 13:31-35 172
John 13:34-35 196
John 14:6 115
John 14:16 49
John 14:27 .... 86, 109, 168
John 15:1 63
John 15:7 151
John 15:11 222
John 15:12 196
John 20:1 121
John 20:19-26 215
John 20:21 212

ACTS
Acts 1:8 75
Acts 2:17 74
Acts 2:39 135
Acts 2:44 154
Acts 4:27 183
Acts 4:32 154
Acts 6:3 6
Acts 7:33 42
Acts 7:36 106
Acts 8:6-8 171
Acts 8:15 142
Acts 9:17 212
Acts 16:14 .... 21, 79
Acts 17:25 103
Acts 17:29 44
Acts 21:14 151

ROMANS

Rom 5:5 100
Rom 5:52 79
Rom 6:9-10 162
Rom 8:11 182
Rom 8:19-21 157
Rom 12:1 18
Rom 12:5 200
Rom 12:6 169
Rom 12:10 196
Rom 12:15 111
Rom 13:8 196
Rom 14:17 146
Rom 15:13 146
Rom 15:13 168

1 CORINTHIANS

1 Cor 3:8 154
1 Cor 4:1 147
1 Cor 6:11-13 79
1 Cor 7:7 169
1 Cor 8:6 141
1 Cor 10:16 .... 173, 200, 202
1 Cor 11:23-26 195
1 Cor 11:24-25 201
1 Cor 11:26 197
1 Cor 12:8 6
1 Cor 12:7-13 154
1 Cor 12:11-13 44
1 Cor 12:12-13 200
1 Cor 12:27 .... 171, 200
1 Cor 12:31 82
1 Cor 13 170
1 Cor 14:15 191
1 Cor 16:13 99
1 Cor 16:22 4

2 CORINTHIANS

2 Cor 1:2 224
2 Cor 4:6 103
2 Cor 4:15 185
2 Cor 5:17 .... 148, 152
2 Cor 6:13 21
2 Cor 6:16 18
2 Cor 12:9 120
2 Cor 13:11 24

GALATIANS

Gal 3:28 .... 141, 159, 178
Gal 5:1 99
Gal 5:13 35
Gal 5:22 .... 24, 101, 146, 222
Gal 6:15 148

EPHESIANS

Eph 1:17 6
Eph 2:18 .... 44, 154
Eph 2:21-22 18
Eph 3:16 218
Eph 3:16-19 119
Eph 3:17 181
Eph 3:18-19 144
Eph 3:19 81
Eph 3:20 182
Eph 4:4 .... 44, 154
Eph 5:9 31
Eph 6:23 24

PHILIPPIANS

Phil 1:27 .... 44, 154
Phil 2:7 47
Phil 2:10 155
Phil 4:1 99
Phil 4:6-9 211
Phil 4:7 224

COLOSSIANS

Col 1:15 44
Col 1:15-16 39
Col 1:15-19 145
Col 1:18 200
Col 3:3 162
Col 3:16 182
Col 4:6 209

1 THESSALONIANS

1 Thess 1:4 11
1 Thess 3:12 196
1 Thess 4:9 .... 89, 196
1 Thess 5:10 103
1 Thess 5:23 224

2 THESSALONIANS

2 Thess 2:13 11
2 Thess 3:16 86

2 TIMOTHY

2 Tim 1:10 162
2 Tim 2:13 182

HEBREWS

Heb 12:28 184
Heb 13:8 38
Heb 13:20 224

JAMES

James 2:5 11
James 5:13 191

1 PETER

1 Peter 1:2 11
1 Peter 1:22 13
1 Peter 1:22-23 196
1 Peter 2:24 91
1 Peter 3:8 .... 44, 154, 196
1 Peter 4:8 196
1 Peter 4:11 34
1 Peter 5:10 119

1 JOHN

1 John 2:8 31
1 John 3:1 35
1 John 3:11-23 196
1 John 3:14 162
1 John 3:16 213
1 John 3:18 13
1 John 4:6-21 107
1 John 4:7 89
1 John 4:7-12 196
1 John 4:9 100

2 JOHN

2 John 3 .... 24, 81
2 John 5 196

JUDE

Jude 2 24
Jude 25 34

REVELATION

Rev 1:8 106
Rev 1:5 91
Rev 3:20 94
Rev 4:8 .... 203, 206
Rev 4:11 34
Rev 5:13 88
Rev 11:17 187
Rev 12:10 140
Rev 19:1 36
Rev 21:4 120
Rev 21:5 .... 49, 199
Rev 21:10 142
Rev 22:1 160
Rev 22:1-2 163
Rev 22:2 .... 5, 135
Rev 22:17 182
Rev 22:17-20 4
Rev 22:20 19

Liturgical Use, Topics, and Categories

Further indices, including a full index of child-friendly repertoire, are available on
the *More Voices* website, www.morevoices.ca

ABUSE
78   God weeps
74   When painful mem'ries haunt

AGING
83   Let my spirit always sing
176 Three things I promise

ANGELS
11   Come, come Emmanuel
158 Dream a dream
190 Laughter lit the stars
212 Sent out in Jesus' name
134 There was a child in Galilee
65   When we are tested

**ANNIVERSARY
(CONGREGATION)**
1   Let us build a house
42   Praise God for this holy ground

**ANNIVERSARY (THE UNITED
CHURCH OF CANADA)**
125 When a grain of wheat

**ASSURANCE (see SERVICE
MUSIC: ASSURANCE)**

BAPTISM
82   Bathe me in your light
115 Behold, I make all things new
117 By the well a thirsty woman
10   Come and seek the ways
16   Confitemini Domino
7   Gather us in, ground us in you
157 I am a child of God
161 I have called you by your name
190 Laughter lit the stars
144 Like a healing stream
214 May God's sheltering wings
163 River running in you and me
75   Veni Sancte Spiritus
93   What calls me from the death

**BENEDICTION
(see SERVICE MUSIC:
SENDING FORTH)**

**CELEBRATION OF
MINISTRIES**
161 I have called you by your name

CENTRING
77   Be still and know
47   Born in human likeness
24   Breath of God, breath of peace
16   Confitemini Domino
91   Cradle me in your arms
86   Da pacem cordium
123 Day after day
7   Gather us in, ground us in you

15   Holy, sacred Spirit
106 I am the dream
189 Jesus, we are here
101 Jesus, you fill our hearts
83   Let my spirit always sing
144 Like a healing stream
14   Where two or three

**CHILDREN (full index at
www.morevoices.ca)**

**CHILDREN – ACTION
SONGS**
48   I can feel you near me, God
183 I'm gonna shout, shout, shout
92   Like a rock
215 Peace be with you
187 We give our hands to you

**CHILDREN – SHORTER
SONGS**
52   Alleluia (Uruguay)
219 Ameni
2   Come, all you people
156 Dance with the Spirit
36   Glory to God/Gloria a Dios
107 God loves me
108 I know your word
210 Jesus, loving Lord
189 Jesus, we are here
104 Know that God is good
214 May God's sheltering wings
122 This is the day
191 What can I do?

**CHILDREN – STORY
SONGS**
121 Hey now! Singing hallelujah!
127 I saw the rich ones
113 Jesus saw them fishing
195 Long ago and far away

**CHILDREN – ZIPPER
SONGS**
221 I am walking a path of peace
183 I'm gonna shout, shout, shout
33   Jesus came bringing us
213 Take up his song
45   You are holy, you show us

**CHRISTIAN YEAR –
ADVENT**
4   All who are thirsty
114 Behold the face of Christ
80   Beyond the beauty and the awe
24   Breath of God, breath of peace
11   Come, come Emmanuel
16   Confitemini Domino
90   Don't be afraid
17   God in the darkness
20   God of still waiting

78   God weeps
220 Hope shines as the solitary star
84   In you there is a refuge
210 Jesus, loving Lord
33   Jesus came bringing us
103 Ka mana'o 'I 'O
83   Let my spirit always sing
144 Like a healing stream
18   Lord, prepare me
81   Love us into fullness
19   Maranatha
222 May the peace of God
175 May we but wait
120 My soul cries out
146 The kingdom of God
134 There was a child in Galilee
75   Veni Sancte Spiritus
137 Welcome, Jesus
169 When hands reach out beyond
74   When painful mem'ries haunt
71   When the wind of winter blows
45   You are holy, you show us
151 Your will be done

**CHRISTIAN YEAR
– CHRISTMAS**
59   Alleluia, praise to God
54   Alleluia (Monteiro)
52   Alleluia (Uruguay)
111 A voice was heard in Ramah
47   Born in human likeness
162 Christ, within us hidden
56   Come, O come, let us praise
158 Dream a dream
36   Glory to God/Gloria a Dios
124 Glory to God in the highest
147 God help us to treasure
182 Grateful for the life you give us
183 I'm gonna shout, shout, shout
33   Jesus came bringing us
166 Jesus Christ, Jesus Christ
97   Listen, God is calling
89   Love is the touch
40   Never ending joy
134 There was a child in Galilee
49   When we seek language

**CHRISTIAN YEAR –
NEW YEAR**
115 Behold, I make all things new
114 Behold the face of Christ

**CHRISTIAN YEAR –
EPIPHANY**
96   And when you call for me
111 A voice was heard in Ramah
82   Bathe me in your light
115 Behold, I make all things new
153 Body, mind and spirit
47   Born in human likeness
117 By the well a thirsty woman

162 Christ, within us hidden
10 Come and seek the ways
145 Draw the circle wide
110 First-born of Mary
209 Go make a diff'rence
211 Go now in peace, guided
172 God says
182 Grateful for the life you give us
220 Hope shines as the solitary star
167 Hush! Hush!
157 I am a child of God
201 I am the bread of life
106 I am the dream
161 I have called you by your name
33 Jesus came bringing us
166 Jesus Christ, Jesus Christ
113 Jesus saw them fishing
190 Laughter lit the stars
144 Like a healing stream
89 Love is the touch
212 Sent out in Jesus' name
213 Take up his song
146 The kingdom of God
151 Your will be done
45 You are holy, you show us

CHRISTIAN YEAR – LENT
140 As long as we follow
114 Behold the face of Christ
77 Be still and know
80 Beyond the beauty and the awe
16 Confitemini Domino
28 God of the Bible
78 God weeps
95 How deep the peace
201 I am the bread of life
76 If I have been the source of pain
84 In you there is a refuge
210 Jesus, loving Lord
166 Jesus Christ, Jesus Christ
133 Jesus laughed out loud
83 Let my spirit always sing
97 Listen, God is calling
18 Lord, prepare me
94 Love knocks and waits
81 Love us into fullness
118 Me alone
73 O God, why are you silent?
66 Senzeni na?
179 Sisters let us walk together
213 Take up his song
75 Veni Sancte Spiritus
125 When a grain of wheat
74 When painful mem'ries haunt
65 When we are tested
45 You are holy, you show us

CHRISTIAN YEAR – PALM SUNDAY
8 And on this path
128 When they heard that Jesus

CHRISTIAN YEAR – HOLY WEEK
64 Because you came
114 Behold the face of Christ

162 Christ, within us hidden
133 Jesus laughed out loud
189 Jesus, we are here

CHRISTIAN YEAR – EASTER
59 Alleluia, praise to God
50 Alleluia (Duncan)
54 Alleluia (Monteiro)
52 Alleluia (Uruguay)
8 And on this path
126 Are you a shepherd?
186 Because Jesus felt
64 Because you came
115 Behold, I make all things new
114 Behold the face of Christ
47 Born in human likeness
171 Christ has no body now
162 Christ, within us hidden
90 Don't be afraid
48 I can feel you near me, God
183 I'm gonna shout, shout, shout
166 Jesus Christ, Jesus Christ
102 Jesus, your Spirit in us
39 Mother Earth, our mother
40 Never ending joy
180 Sing, sing out! Sing a new song
122 This is the day that God has made
58 We sing of your glory
125 When a grain of wheat
49 When we seek language
14 Where two or three
45 You are holy, you show us

CHRISTIAN YEAR – GOOD SHEPHERD SUNDAY
126 Are you a shepherd?

CHRISTIAN YEAR – ASCENSION
171 Christ has no body now
162 Christ, within us hidden
183 I'm gonna shout, shout, shout
102 Jesus, your Spirit in us

CHRISTIAN YEAR – PENTECOST
4 All who are thirsty
64 Because you came
24 Breath of God, breath of peace
135 Called by earth and sky
156 Dance with the Spirit
20 God of still waiting
15 Holy sacred Spirit
6 Holy Spirit, come into our lives
161 I have called you by your name
102 Jesus, your Spirit in us
144 Like a healing stream
98 Like a river of tears
25 O God, send out your Spirit
13 O let the power fall on me
142 Oh, a song must rise
150 Spirit God, be our breath
75 Veni Sancte Spiritus

87 Water flowing
49 When we seek language

CHRISTIAN YEAR – TRINITY SUNDAY
56 Come, O come, let us praise
43 The play of the Godhead
49 When we seek language

CHRISTIAN YEAR – THANKSGIVING (see THANKSGIVING)

CHRISTIAN YEAR – ALL SAINTS
112 Amen, Amen, it shall be so

CHRISTIAN YEAR – REIGN OF CHRIST
114 Behold the face of Christ
162 Christ within us hidden

CHURCH DEDICATION
1 Let us build a house

COMMISSIONING (see SERVICE MUSIC: SENDING FORTH)

COMMITMENT
179 Sisters let us walk together
99 Stand, O stand firm
213 Take up his song
165 There is a time
176 Three things I promise
196 We will take what you offer

COMMUNITY
153 Body, mind and spirit
56 Come, O come, let us praise
154 Deep in our hearts
145 Draw the circle wide
7 Gather us in, ground us in you
147 God help us to treasure
53 God who spread the boundless
127 I saw the rich ones
159 In star and crescent
103 Ka mana'o 'I 'O
195 Long ago and far away
181 Lord, your hands have formed
62 There is room for all
14 Where two or three
178 Who is my mother

CONFIRMATION
161 I have called you by your name
63 Long before my journey's start
85 Take, O take me as I am

CONSECRATION
80 Beyond the beauty and the awe
117 By the well a thirsty woman

CONTEMPLATIVE PRAYER
80 Beyond the beauty and the awe

153 Body, mind and spirit
16 Confitemini Domino
91 Cradle me in your arms
90 Don't be afraid
7 Gather us in, ground us in you
17 God in the darkness
172 God says
15 Holy, sacred Spirit
106 I am the dream
84 In you there is a refuge
101 Jesus, you fill our hearts
102 Jesus, your Spirit in us

COVENANTING
10 Come and seek the ways
27 Creator God, you gave us life
107 God loves me
157 I am a child of God of God
161 I have called you by your name
1 Let us build a house
212 Sent out in Jesus' name

CREATION
135 Called by earth and sky
10 Come and seek the ways
27 Creator God, you gave us life
123 Day after day
158 Dream a dream
37 Each blade of grass
172 God says
53 God who spread the boundless
217 Hey ney yana
35 Holy One, O Holy One
15 Holy sacred Spirit
30 It's a song of praise
103 Ka mana'o 'I 'O
190 Laughter lit the stars
144 Like a healing stream
98 Like a river of tears
92 Like a rock
181 Lord, your hands have formed
39 Mother Earth, our mother
41 O beautiful Gaia
42 Praise God for this holy ground
173 Put peace into each other's
163 River running in you and me
180 Sing, sing out! Sing a new song
174 Soil of God, you and I
43 The play of the Godhead
55 Watch once more the
    wind swept
87 Water flowing
141 We are all one people
143 We cannot own the sunlit sky
125 When a grain of wheat
198 When we gather at the table
131 You, Creator God,
    have searched
152 You who watch the highest

CREATIVITY
27 Creator God, you gave us life

DARKNESS
147 God help us to treasure
17 God in the darkness

214 May God's sheltering wings
109 My soul is thirsting for you
44 Shadow and substance
62 There is room for all
131 You, Creator God,
    have searched

**DEDICATION (see
CONSECRATION)**

**DISABILITY
(SEE DIVERSITY)**

DISCERNMENT
96 And when you call for me
194 Bread of life, feed my soul
117 By the well a thirsty woman
135 Called by earth and sky
162 Christ, within us hidden
10 Come and seek the ways
11 Come, come Emmanuel
123 Day after day
7 Gather us in, ground us in you
20 God of still waiting
172 God says
78 God weeps
15 Holy sacred Spirit
6 Holy Spirit, come into our lives
148 Hope of Abraham and Sarah
167 Hush! Hush!
221 I am walking a path of peace
161 I have called you by your name
108 I know your word
84 In you there is a refuge
133 Jesus laughed out loud
113 Jesus saw them fishing
83 Let my spirit always sing
144 Like a healing stream
98 Like a river of tears
97 Listen, God is calling
63 Long before my journey's start
18 Lord, prepare me
94 Love knocks and waits
81 Love us into fullness
175 May we but wait
118 Me alone
138 My love colours outside
109 My soul is thirsting for you
163 River running in you and me
3 River, rush-a-down to the ocean
79 Spirit, open my heart
99 Stand, O stand firm
85 Take, O take me as I am
165 There is a time
139 True faith needs no defence
75 Veni Sancte Spiritus
125 When a grain of wheat
65 When we are tested
14 Where two or three
45 You are holy, you show us
151 Your will be done

DISCIPLESHIP
11 Come, come Emmanuel
156 Dance with the Spirit
110 First-born of Mary

209 Go make a diff'rence
147 God help us to treasure
172 God says
53 God who spread the boundless
6 Holy Spirit, come into our lives
167 Hush! Hush!!
157 I am a child of God of God
161 I have called you by your name
183 I'm gonna shout, shout, shout
133 Jesus laughed out loud
113 Jesus saw them fishing
103 Ka mana'o 'I 'O
195 Long ago and far away
18 Lord, prepare me
212 Sent out in Jesus' name
213 Take up his song
176 Three things I promise
196 We will take what you offer

DIVERSITY
27 Creator God, you gave us life
136 When hands reach out
    and fingers
178 Who is my mother

ECOLOGY (see CREATION)

ETERNAL LIFE
113 Jesus saw them fishing
102 Jesus, your Spirit in us

EVENING
123 Day after day
17 God in the darkness
217 Hey ney yana
210 Jesus, loving Lord
103 Ka mana'o 'I 'O

FAITH
82 Bathe me in your light
162 Christ within us hidden
20 God of still waiting
220 Hope shines as the solitary star
139 True faith needs no defence
199 When at this table I receive

FAITHFULNESS
186 Because Jesus felt
28 God of the Bible
182 Grateful for the life you give us
183 I'm gonna shout, shout, shout
103 Ka mana'o 'I 'O

FIRST NATIONS SUNDAY
37 Each blade of grass
217 Hey ney yana
141 We are all one people

FORGIVENESS
64 Because you came
95 How deep the peace
76 If I have been the source of pain
97 Listen, God is calling
89 Love is the touch
81 Love us into fullness
160 There's a river of life

FUNERALS AND MEMORIAL SERVICES
(see also LAMENT)
17 God in the darkness
125 When a grain of wheat

GOD: IMAGES
126 Are you a shepherd?
49 When we seek language
105 You are my Father

GOD: PRESENCE
103 Ka mana'o 'I 'O
83 Let my spirit always sing
92 Like a rock

GRACE
82 Bathe me in your light
12 Come touch our hearts
98 Like a river of tears
81 Love us into fullness
79 Spirit, open my heart
139 True faith needs no defence
136 When hands reach out
    and fingers

GRATITUDE
182 Grateful for the life
    you give us
188 I thank you, thank you, Jesus

**GRIEF (see ABUSE,
FUNERALS, LAMENT)**

HEALING
4 All who are thirsty
112 Amen, Amen, it shall be so
96 And when you call for me
82 Bathe me in your light
186 Because Jesus felt
115 Behold, I make all things new
80 Beyond the beauty and the awe
46 Bless the Lord
153 Body, mind and spirit
194 Bread of life, feed my soul
24 Breath of God, breath of peace
117 By the well a thirsty woman
171 Christ has no body now
10 Come and seek the ways
16 Confitemini Domino
91 Cradle me in your arms
19 Don't be afraid
147 God help us to treasure
17 God in the darkness
20 God of still waiting
28 God of the Bible
119 God our protector
78 God weeps
132 Great sorrow prodded Jairus
6 Holy Spirit, come into our lives
5 Holy Spirit, you're like
    the wind
95 How deep the peace
157 I am a child of God
84 In you there is a refuge

210 Jesus, loving Lord
101 Jesus, you fill our hearts
103 Ka mana'o 'I 'O
83 Let my spirit always sing
1 Let us build a house
144 Like a healing stream
98 Like a river of tears
97 Listen, God is calling
195 Long ago and far away
63 Long before my journey's start
100 Lord God, you love us
89 Love is the touch
94 Love knocks and waits
81 Love us into fullness
19 Maranatha
214 May God's sheltering wings
118 Me alone
109 My soul is thirsting for you
73 O God, why are you silent?
163 River running in you and me
3 River, rush-a-down to the ocean
179 Sisters let us walk together
150 Spirit God, be our breath
75 Veni Sancte Spiritus
87 Water flowing
137 Welcome, Jesus
93 What calls me from the death
125 When a grain of wheat
74 When painful mem'ries haunt
128 When they heard that Jesus
72 Why stand so far away

HEALTH/WELLNESS
153 Body, mind and spirit
132 Great sorrow prodded Jairus
83 Let my spirit always sing
136 When hands reach out
    and fingers

HOLY SPIRIT
23 Come, O holy Spirit
156 Dance with the Spirit
15 Holy sacred Spirit
6 Holy Spirit, come into our lives
5 Holy Spirit, you're like
    the wind
144 Like a healing stream
25 O God, send out your Spirit
13 O let the power fall on me
142 Oh, a song must rise
163 River running in you and me
3 River, rush-a-down to
    the ocean
79 Spirit, open my heart
150 Spirit God, be our breath
155 Unbounded Spirit, breath
    of God
75 Veni Sancte Spiritus
87 Water flowing

HOPE
140 As long as we follow
28 God of the Bible
148 Hope of Abraham and Sarah
220 Hope shines as the solitary star
33 Jesus came bringing us hope

83 Let my spirit always sing
116 The thirsty deer
9 Venite, exultemus Domino
169 When hands reach out beyond

INCLUSIVENESS
145 Draw the circle wide
159 In star and crescent
62 There is room for all
136 When hands reach out
    and fingers

INSPIRATION
24 Breath of God, breath of peace
123 Day after day
110 First-born of Mary
102 Jesus, your Spirit in us
49 When we seek language

INTERFAITH
154 Deep in our hearts
148 Hope of Abraham and Sarah
159 In star and crescent
142 Oh, a song must rise
173 Put peace into each other's
141 We are all one people
105 You are my Father
169 When hands reach out beyond

INVOCATION
4 All who are thirsty
24 Breath of God, breath of peace
23 Come, O holy Spirit
20 God of still waiting
5 Holy Spirit, you're like
    the wind
25 O God, send out your Spirit
13 O let the power fall on me
14 Where two or three

JESUS CHRIST
186 Because Jesus felt
114 Behold the face of Christ
47 Born in human likeness
117 By the well a thirsty woman
162 Christ, within us hidden
11 Come, come Emmanuel
91 Cradle me in your arms
110 First-born of Mary
38 Glory to God/Nzamuranza
132 Great sorrow prodded Jairus
121 Hey now! Singing hallelujah!
201 I am the bread of life
127 I saw the rich ones
188 I thank you, thank you, Jesus
183 I'm gonna shout, shout, shout
33 Jesus came bringing us
166 Jesus Christ, Jesus Christ
133 Jesus laughed out loud
210 Jesus, loving Lord
113 Jesus saw them fishing
189 Jesus, we are here
101 Jesus, you fill our hearts
102 Jesus, your Spirit in us
195 Long ago and far away
81 Love us into fullness

19   Maranatha
118   Me alone
177   This is my body
137   Welcome, Jesus
128   When they heard that Jesus

JESUS CHRIST: INCARNATION
114   Behold the face of Christ
47   Born in human likeness

JESUS CHRIST: CROSS
64   Because you came
162   Christ within us hidden
28   God of the Bible
121   Hey now! Singing hallelujah!
133   Jesus laughed out loud
113   Jesus saw them fishing
1   Let us build a house
73   O God, why are you silent?

JESUS CHRIST: RESURRECTION
64   Because you came
114   Behold the face of Christ
162   Christ within us hidden
121   Hey now! Singing hallelujah!
125   When a grain of wheat

JESUS CHRIST: SECOND COMING
4   All who are thirsty
19   Maranatha
151   Your will be done

JOURNEY
8   And on this path
82   Bathe me in your light
202   Bread for the journey
156   Dance with the Spirit
145   Draw the circle wide
220   Hope shines as the solitary star
106   I am the dream
221   I am walking a path of peace
159   In star and crescent
63   Long before my journey's start
89   Love is the touch
81   Love us into fullness
216   Wherever you may go
45   You are holy, you show us

JOY
157   I am a child of God
48   I can feel you near me, God
183   I'm gonna shout, shout, shout
133   Jesus laughed out loud
190   Laughter lit the stars
83   Let my spirit always sing
98   Like a river of tears
97   Listen, God is calling
89   Love is the touch
222   May the peace of God
39   Mother Earth, our mother
120   My soul cries out
40   Never ending joy
180   Sing, sing out! Sing a new song

62   There is room for all
134   There was a child in Galilee
122   This is the day that God has made
223   We will go with God

JUSTICE
111   A voice was heard in Ramah
112   Amen, Amen, it shall be so
140   As long as we follow
114   Behold the face of Christ
46   Bless the Lord
117   By the well a thirsty woman
135   Called by earth and sky
171   Christ has no body now
10   Come and seek the ways
156   Dance with the Spirit
154   Deep in our hearts
145   Draw the circle wide
158   Dream a dream
110   First-born of Mary
193   God bless to us our bread
28   God of the Bible
172   God says
78   God weeps
209   Go make a diff'rence
132   Great sorrow prodded Jairus
6   Holy Spirit, come into our lives
148   Hope of Abraham and Sarah
157   I am a child of God
161   I have called you by your name
127   I saw the rich ones
76   If I have been the source of pain
1   Let us build a house
144   Like a healing stream
195   Long ago and far away
19   Maranatha
120   My soul cries out
25   O God, send out your Spirit
13   O let the power fall on me
142   Oh, a song must rise
149   Peace for the children
31   Pure love
212   Sent out in Jesus' name
179   Sisters let us walk together
146   The kingdom of God
134   There was a child in Galilee
143   We cannot own the sunlit sky
137   Welcome, Jesus
199   When at this table I receive
169   When hands reach out beyond
128   When they heard that Jesus
198   When we gather at the table
72   Why stand so far away
151   Your will be done

KINGDOM
140   As long as we follow
80   Beyond the beauty and the awe
171   Christ has no body now
156   Dance with the Spirit
154   Deep in our hearts
158   Dream a dream
53   God who spread the boundless
127   I saw the rich ones

89   Love is the touch
222   May the peace of God
212   Sent out in Jesus' name
146   The kingdom of God
143   We cannot own the sunlit sky
151   Your will be done

KYRIES (see also SERVICE MUSIC: CONFESSION)
11   Come, come Emmanuel
67   Kyrie (Bridget)
68   Kyrie (Guarani)
69   Kyrie (Kervin)
70   Kyrie (Reindorf)

LAMENT
111   A voice was heard in Ramah
78   God weeps
73   O God, why are you silent?
72   Why stand so far away

LEARNING
12   Come touch our hearts
123   Day after day
148   Hope of Abraham and Sarah
136   When hands reach out and fingers

LIFE TRANSITIONS
63   Long before my journey's start

LIGHT
82   Bathe me in your light
80   Beyond the beauty and the awe
135   Called by earth and sky
10   Come and seek the ways
28   God of the Bible
209   Go make a diff'rence
211   Go now in peace, guided
6   Holy Spirit, come into our lives
5   Holy Spirit, you're like the wind
220   Hope shines as the solitary star
108   I know your word
84   In you there is a refuge
109   My soul is thirsting for you
155   Unbounded Spirit, breath of God
137   Welcome, Jesus
71   When the wind of winter blows
131   You, Creator God, have searched

LOVE
35   Holy One, O Holy One
103   Ka mana'o 'I 'O
190   Laughter lit the stars
89   Love is the touch
94   Love knocks and waits
138   My love colours outside
31   Pure love
169   When hands reach out beyond

LOVE FOR GOD/CHRIST
(see also PRAISE, THANKS-GIVING)
46 Bless the Lord
182 Grateful for the life you give us
188 I thank you, thank you, Jesus
183 I'm gonna shout, shout, shout

LOVE FOR OTHERS
179 Sisters let us walk together
165 There is a time
170 Ubi caritas
136 When hands reach out
 and fingers
216 Wherever you may go
178 Who is my mother

LOVE OF GOD/CHRIST
91 Cradle me in your arms
90 Don't be afraid
107 God loves me
60 God, we give you heartfelt
166 Jesus Christ, Jesus Christ
101 Jesus, you fill our hearts
98 Like a river of tears
100 Lord God, you love us
81 Love us into fullness
214 May God's sheltering wings
62 There is room for all
176 Three things I promise
49 When we seek language
131 You, Creator God,
 have searched
26 Your love is amazing
 (Hallelujah)

MARRIAGE
35 Holy One, O Holy One
89 Love is the touch
216 Wherever you may go

MEAL GRACE
194 Bread of life, feed my soul
193 God bless to us our bread

MYSTERY
153 Body, mind and spirit
27 Creator God, you gave us life
158 Dream a dream
147 God help us to treasure
17 God in the darkness
106 I am the dream
44 Shadow and substance

NATIONAL DAY OF ACTION
78 God weeps

NATIONHOOD
53 God who spread the boundless

NURTURE
91 Cradle me in your arms
90 Don't be afraid
211 Go now in peace, guided
107 God loves me

119 God our protector
35 Holy One, O Holy One
48 I can feel you near me, God
84 In you there is a refuge
190 Laughter lit the stars
83 Let my spirit always sing
195 Long ago and far away
214 May God's sheltering wings
62 There is room for all

OBEDIENCE
212 Sent out in Jesus' name
213 Take up his song
176 Three things I promise
196 We will take what you offer

PEACE
111 A voice was heard in Ramah
64 Because you came
80 Beyond the beauty and the awe
171 Christ has no body now
6 Holy Spirit, come into our lives
148 Hope of Abraham and Sarah
221 I am walking a path of peace
1 Let us build a house
168 May Peace be with you
224 May the God of peace
222 May the peace of God
215 Peace be with you
149 Peace for the children
173 Put peace into each other's
143 We cannot own the sunlit sky
169 When hands reach out beyond

PRAISE
59 Alleluia, praise to God
50 Alleluia (Duncan)
54 Alleluia (Monteiro)
52 Alleluia (Uruguay)
47 Born in human likeness
2 Come all you people/
 Uyai Mose
56 Come, O come, let us praise
185 Ev'ry day is a day
60 God, we give you heartfelt
32 Hallelujah (Pattison)
29 How lovely is your dwelling
48 I can feel you near me, God
61 I praise you, O God
57 I'll praise eternal God
183 I'm gonna shout, shout, shout
30 It's a song of praise
203 O holy, holy, holy God
42 Praise God for this holy ground
58 We sing of your glory
49 When we seek language
51 Yahweh be praised
131 You, Creator God,
 have searched

QUIET
84 In you there is a refuge
103 Ka mana'o 'I 'O
139 True faith needs no defence

RAINBOWS
165 There is a time

REDEMPTION
17 God in the darkness
133 Jesus laughed out loud
97 Listen, God is calling
94 Love knocks and waits
81 Love us into fullness
49 When we seek language

REMEMBRANCE DAY
111 A voice was heard in Ramah
78 God weeps
148 Hope of Abraham and Sarah
149 Peace for the children

RENEWAL
17 God in the darkness
15 Holy sacred Spirit
144 Like a healing stream
98 Like a river of tears
18 Lord, prepare me
181 Lord, your hands have formed
94 Love knocks and waits
93 What calls me from the death
125 When a grain of wheat

RENEWAL OF BAPTISMAL VOWS
117 By the well a thirsty woman
157 I am a child of God
161 I have called you by your name
190 Laughter lit the stars

RESURRECTION (see also JESUS CHRIST: RESURRECTION)
125 When a grain of wheat
93 What calls me from the death

RURAL LIFE
181 Lord, your hands have formed

SEASONS
181 Lord, your hands have formed
43 The play of the Godhead

SERVICE MUSIC: GATHERING
59 Alleluia, praise to God
4 All who are thirsty
8 And on this path
115 Behold, I make all things new
77 Be still and know
46 Bless the Lord
24 Breath of God, breath of peace
135 Called by earth and sky
10 Come and seek the ways
11 Come, come Emmanuel
56 Come, O come, let us praise
16 Confitemini Domino
156 Dance with the Spirit
123 Day after day
158 Dream a dream
185 Ev'ry day is a day

7 Gather us in, ground us in you
147 God help us to treasure
17 God in the darkness
22 God of all the world
172 God says
60 God, we give you heartfelt
53 God who spread the boundless
182 Grateful for the life you give us
15 Holy sacred Spirit
6 Holy Spirit, come into our lives
29 How lovely is your dwelling
57 I'll praise eternal God
183 I'm gonna shout, shout, shout
61 I praise you, O God
30 It's a song of praise
189 Jesus, we are here
97 Listen, God is calling
18 Lord, prepare me
94 Love knocks and waits
19 Maranatha
109 My soul is thirsting for you
25 O God, send out your Spirit
142 Oh, a song must rise
146 The kingdom of God
43 The play of the Godhead
75 Veni Sancte Spiritus
137 Welcome, Jesus
178 Who is my mother

SERVICE MUSIC:
CONFESSION
64 Because you came
114 Behold the face of Christ
24 Breath of God, breath of peace
11 Come, come Emmanuel
17 God in the darkness
20 God of still waiting
78 God weeps
5 Holy Spirit, you're like
   the wind
76 If I have been the source of pain
67 Kyrie eleison (Bridget)
68 Kyrie eleison (Guarani)
69 Kyrie eleison (Kervin)
83 Let my spirit always sing
19 Maranatha
118 Me alone
109 My soul is thirsting for you
66 Senzeni na?
93 What calls me from the death
125 When a grain of wheat
74 When painful mem'ries haunt
71 When the wind of winter blows
65 When we are tested

SERVICE MUSIC:
ASSURANCE
96 And when you call for me
140 As long as we follow
186 Because Jesus felt
64 Because you came
115 Behold, I make all things new
114 Behold the face of Christ
77 Be still and know
46 Bless the Lord

153 Body, mind and spirit
91 Cradle me in your arms
90 Don't be afraid
185 Ev'ry day is a day
36 Glory to God/Gloria a Dios
107 God loves me
28 God of the Bible
119 God our protector
60 God, we give you heartfelt
95 How deep the peace
157 I am a child of God
48 I can feel you near me, God
188 I thank you, thank you, Jesus
57 I'll praise eternal God
183 I'm gonna shout, shout, shout
84 In you there is a refuge
33 Jesus came bringing us
166 Jesus Christ, Jesus Christ
101 Jesus, you fill our hearts
102 Jesus, your Spirit in us
103 Ka mana'o 'I 'O
144 Like a healing stream
98 Like a river of tears
92 Like a rock
97 Listen, God is calling
63 Long before my journey's start
100 Lord God, you love us
18 Lord, prepare me
89 Love is the touch
81 Love us into fullness
214 May God's sheltering wings
40 Never ending joy
125 When a grain of wheat
105 You are my Father

SERVICE MUSIC: PRAYER
FOR ILLUMINATION/
SCRIPTURE RESPONSE
112 Amen, Amen, it shall be so
8 And on this path
186 Because Jesus felt
114 Behold the face of Christ
80 Beyond the beauty and the awe
24 Breath of God, breath of peace
10 Come and seek the ways
11 Come, come Emmanuel
16 Confitemini Domino
123 Day after day
110 First-born of Mary
172 God says
15 Holy sacred Spirit
6 Holy Spirit, come into our lives
201 I am the bread of life
108 I know your word
183 I'm gonna shout, shout, shout
127 I saw the rich ones
166 Jesus Christ, Jesus Christ
189 Jesus, we are here
102 Jesus, your Spirit in us
97 Listen, God is calling
63 Long before my journey's start
175 May we but wait
31 Pure love
146 The kingdom of God
196 We will take what you offer

125 When a grain of wheat
178 Who is my mother

SERVICE MUSIC:
RESPONSE/AFFIRMATION
112 Amen, Amen, it shall be so
96 And when you call for me
184 Ay, ay, salidummay
186 Because Jesus felt
115 Behold, I make all things new
114 Behold the face of Christ
77 Be still and know
80 Beyond the beauty and the awe
46 Bless the Lord
47 Born in human likeness
171 Christ has no body now
162 Christ, within us hidden
27 Creator God, you gave us life
123 Day after day
154 Deep in our hearts
90 Don't be afraid
145 Draw the circle wide
158 Dream a dream
185 Ev'ry day is a day
110 First-born of Mary
36 Glory to God/Gloria a Dios
172 God says
53 God who spread the boundless
209 Go make a diff'rence
182 Grateful for the life you give us
167 Hush! Hush!
157 I am a child of God
106 I am the dream
48 I can feel you near me, God
161 I have called you by your name
61 I praise you, O God
188 I thank you, thank you, Jesus
183 I'm gonna shout, shout, shout
30 It's a song of praise
33 Jesus came bringing us
133 Jesus laughed out loud
113 Jesus saw them fishing
189 Jesus, we are here
101 Jesus, you fill our hearts
102 Jesus, your Spirit in us
103 Ka mana'o 'I 'O
83 Let my spirit always sing
144 Like a healing stream
98 Like a river of tears
92 Like a rock
97 Listen, God is calling
18 Lord, prepare me
181 Lord, your hands have formed
89 Love is the touch
81 Love us into fullness
19 Maranatha
214 May God's sheltering wings
40 Never ending joy
173 Put peace into each other's
150 Spirit God, be our breath
213 Take up his song
136 When hands reach out
   and fingers
178 Who is my mother
105 You are my Father
151 Your will be done

SERVICE MUSIC: PRAYER RESPONSES
112 Amen, Amen, it shall be so
96 And when you call for me
175 May we but wait

SERVICE MUSIC: PASSING THE PEACE
7 Gather us in, ground us in you
95 How deep the peace
157 I am a child of God
221 I am walking a path of peace
168 May peace be with you
222 May the peace of God
215 Peace be with you
31 Pure love
173 Put peace into each other's
141 We are all one people

SERVICE MUSIC: OFFERING
54 Alleluia (Monteiro)
34 All is done for the glory
184 Ay, ay, salidummay
115 Behold, I make all things new
135 Called by earth and sky
171 Christ has no body now
56 Come, O come, let us praise
27 Creator God, you gave us life
156 Dance with the Spirit
145 Draw the circle wide
37 Each blade of grass
185 Ev'ry day is a day
28 God of the Bible
60 God, we give you heartfelt
182 Grateful for the life you give us
217 Hey ney yana
61 I praise you, O God
188 I thank you, thank you, Jesus
57 I'll praise eternal God
159 In star and crescent
30 It's a song of praise
166 Jesus Christ, Jesus Christ
133 Jesus laughed out loud
113 Jesus saw them fishing
190 Laughter lit the stars
100 Lord God, you love us
181 Lord, your hands have formed
89 Love is the touch
40 Never ending joy
142 Oh, a song must rise
146 The kingdom of God
191 What can I do?
136 When hands reach out and fingers
178 Who is my mother

SERVICE MUSIC: COMMUNION
4 All who are thirsty
184 Ay, ay, salidummay
80 Beyond the beauty and the awe
47 Born in human likeness
202 Bread for the journey
194 Bread of life, feed my soul

197 Bread of life/Pain de Vie
162 Christ, within us hidden
12 Come touch our hearts
86 Da pacem cordium
90 Don't be afraid
7 Gather us in, ground us in you
193 God, bless to us our bread
147 God help us to treasure
15 Holy, sacred Spirit
201 I am the bread of life
57 I'll praise eternal God
102 Jesus, your Spirit in us
104 Know that God is good
1 Let us build a house
195 Long ago and far away
18 Lord, prepare me
19 Maranatha
21 Open our hearts
173 Put peace into each other's
146 The kingdom of God
62 There is room for all
170 Ubi caritas
192 We come now to your table, Lord
196 We will take what you offer
125 When a grain of wheat
199 When at this table I receive
198 When we gather at the table
14 Where two or three

SERVICE MUSIC: COMMUNION – GREAT THANKSGIVING
47 Born in human likeness

SERVICE MUSIC: COMMUNION – SANCTUS
59 Alleluia, praise to God
36 Glory to God/Gloria a Dios
206 Holy, holy, holy, God of power
57 I'll praise eternal God
104 Know that God is good
203 O holy, holy, holy God
49 When we seek language (refrain)

SERVICE MUSIC: COMMUNION – MEMORIAL ACCLAMATION
207 Christ has died, Christ is risen
19 Maranatha
204 Sing Christ has died

SERVICE MUSIC: SENDING FORTH
140 As long as we follow
202 Bread for the journey
171 Christ has no body now
56 Come, O come, let us praise
86 Da pacem cordium
156 Dance with the Spirit
154 Deep in our hearts
90 Don't be afraid
145 Draw the circle wide

158 Dream a dream
209 Go make a diff'rence
211 Go now in peace, guided
147 God help us to treasure
172 God says
53 God who spread the boundless
182 Grateful for the life you give us
217 Hey ney yana
15 Holy, sacred Spirit
220 Hope shines as the solitary star
221 I am walking a path of peace
161 I have called you by your name
127 I saw the rich ones
188 I thank you, thank you, Jesus
183 I'm gonna shout, shout, shout
210 Jesus, loving Lord
102 Jesus, your Spirit in us
113 Jesus saw them fishing
103 Ka mana'o 'I 'O
144 Like a healing stream
92 Like a rock
63 Long before my journey's start
89 Love is the touch
81 Love us into fullness
214 May God's sheltering wings
168 May peace be with you
224 May the God of peace
218 May the love of the Lord
222 May the peace of God
215 Peace be with you
42 Praise God for this holy ground
173 Put peace into each other's
212 Sent out in Jesus' name
179 Sisters let us walk together
150 Spirit God, be our breath
85 Take, O take me as I am
213 Take up his song
223 We will go with God
196 We will take what you offer
191 What can I do?
216 Wherever you may go
45 You are holy, you show us
151 Your will be done

SERVICE MUSIC: AMEN
225 Amen (Jiang)
205 Amen (Kingsfold)
208 Amen (Patriquin)
112 Amen, Amen, it shall be so
219 Ameni

SPIRITUAL GROWTH
10 Come and seek the ways

STEWARDSHIP
181 Lord, your hands have formed
187 We give our hands to you

TEACHING
126 Are you a shepherd?
1 Let us build a house
155 Unbounded Spirit, breath of God

TEMPTATION
64   Because you came
76   If I have been the source of pain
118 Me alone
65   When we are tested

THANKSGIVING
59   Alleluia, praise to God
54   Alleluia (Monteiro)
34   All is done for the glory
8   And on this path
184 Ay, ay, salidummay
186 Because Jesus felt
46   Bless the Lord
56   Come, O come, let us praise
185 Ev'ry day is a day
107 God loves me
60   God, we give you heartfelt
182 Grateful for the life you give us
217 Hey ney yana
188 I thank you, thank you, Jesus
166 Jesus Christ, Jesus Christ
190 Laughter lit the stars
18   Lord, prepare me
40   Never ending joy
203 O holy, holy, holy God
     (Sanctus)
42   Praise God for this holy ground
43   The play of the Godhead
187 We give our thanks to God
128 When they heard that Jesus
49   When we seek language

TRANSFORMATION
115 Behold, I make all things new
117 By the well a thirsty woman
10   Come and seek the ways

23   Come, O holy Spirit
91   Cradle me in your arms
6   Holy Spirit, come into our lives
144 Like a healing stream
150 Spirit God, be our breath
87   Water flowing
93   What calls me from the death

TRINITY
80   Beyond the beauty and the awe
56   Come, O come, let us praise
10   Come and seek the ways
20   God of still waiting
28   God of the Bible
53   God who spread the boundless
182 Grateful for the life you give us
161 I have called you by your name
30   It's a song of praise
89   Love is the touch
42   Praise God for this holy ground
43   The play of the Godhead
176 Three things I promise
199 When at this table I receive
136 When hands reach out
     and fingers
49   When we seek language

TRUST
95   How deep the peace
29   How lovely is your dwelling
157 I am a child of God
106 I am the dream
161 I have called you by your name
84   In you there is a refuge
83   Let my spirit always sing
62   There is room for all

UNION WITH GOD/CHRIST
162 Christ within us hidden
106 I am the dream
18   Lord, prepare me

UNITY
53   God who spread the boundless
159 In star and crescent
141 We are all one people

URBAN LIFE
80   Beyond the beauty and the awe

VIOLENCE
78   God weeps
179 Sisters let us walk together

WATER
144 Like a healing stream
98   Like a river of tears
163 River running in you and me
3   River, rush-a-down to the ocean
55   Watch once more the
     windswept
87   Water flowing

WINTER
17   God in the darkness
83   Let my spirit always sing
71   When the wind of winter blows

WISDOM
10   Come and seek the ways
6   Holy Spirit, come into our lives
195 Long ago and far away
63   Long before my journey's start

First Lines and Titles
First lines of all languages for each song are included. Song titles are in italics.

142 A Song Must Rise
58   À toi soit la gloire
111 A voice was heard in Ramah
143 *Abundant Life*
59   Aleluya Y'in Oluwa
1   *All Are Welcome*
34   All is done for the glory of
     God
141 *All One People*
4   All who are thirsty
59   Alleluia, praise to God
50   Alleluia (Duncan)
54   Alleluia (Monteiro)
52   Alleluia (Uruguay)
112 Amen, Amen, it shall be so
225 Amen (Jiang)
208 Amen (Patriquin)
205 Amen, Amen, O Holy One
219 Ameni
8   And on this path

96   And when you call for me
126 Are you a shepherd?
140 As long as we follow
188 Asante sana Yesu
88   Aud'ssus de moi, c'est
     d'la musique que j'entends
184 Ay, ay, salidummay
82   Bathe me in your light
1   Bâttisons un lieu d'amour,
     de foi
77   Be still and know
186 Because Jesus felt a woman
     touch his coat
64   Because you came
115 Behold, I make all things new
114 Behold the face of Christ
193 Bendice, Señor, nuestro pan
91   Berce-moi en tes bras
29   *Better Is One Day in
     Your House*

80   Beyond the beauty and the awe
46   Bless the Lord
153 Body, mind and spirit
47   Born in human likeness
202 Bread for the journey
197 Bread of life, broken
     and shared
194 Bread of life, feed my soul
24   Breath of God, breath of peace
117 By the well a thirsty woman
135 Called by earth and sky
120 *Canticle of the Turning*
176 Ce que je promets, ô Dieu saint
104 C'est vrai: Dieu est bon!
62   Chacun a sa place
207 Christ has died, Christ is risen
171 Christ has no body now
     but yours
162 Christ, within us hidden
164 Christe, lux mundi

102 Christus, dein Geist wohnt in uns
60 Chú goán kámsia oló Lí
37 *Circle of God*
2 Come all you people
16 Come and fill our hearts
10 Come and seek the ways of Wisdom
11 Come, come Emmanuel
56 Come, O come, let us praise
23 Come, O Holy Spirit
12 *Come Touch and Bless*
12 Come touch our hearts that we may know compassion
116 Comme un cerf soupire après l'eau
16 Confitemini Domino
91 Cradle me in your arms
27 Creator God, you gave us life
86 Da pacem cordium
156 Dance with the Spirit
123 Day after day
154 Deep in our hearts
193 Dieu, bénis notre pain
90 Don't be afraid
145 Draw the circle wide
158 Dream a dream
134 *Dreaming Mary*
135 Du ciel et de la terre
37 Each blade of grass
107 Elolo nye Mawu elolo nguto
150 *Embracing Change*
212 Enviado soy de Dios
108 Es tu Palabra lampara
96 Et lorsque tu m'appelles
185 Ev'ry day is a day of thanksgiving
195 *Fill the Cup*
110 First-born of Mary
113 *Fish with Me*
28 *Fresh as the Morning*
7 Gather us in, ground us in you
86 Give peace to ev'ry heart
36 Gloire à Dieu
36 Gloria a Dios
36 Glory to God
38 Glory to God/Nzamuranza
124 Glory to God in the highest
209 Go make a diff'rence
211 Go now in peace, guided by the light
193 God bless to us our bread
147 God help us to treasure
17 God in the darkness
107 God loves me, for my God is love
22 God of all the world
20 God of still waiting
28 God of the Bible, God in the Gospel
119 God our protector
172 God says
60 God, we give you heartfelt praise

78 God weeps
53 God who spread the boundless prairie
182 *Grateful*
205 *Great Amen* (Kingsfold)
208 *Great Amen* (Patriquin)
132 Great sorrow prodded Jairus
32 Hallelujah (Pattison)
26 *Hallelujah! (Your Love Is Amazing)*
45 Hamba nathi mkululi wethu
173 *Hands Shaped Like a Cradle*
217 Hey ney yana
121 Hey now! Singing hallelujah!
125 Hitotsubu no
174 *Holy Ground*
206 Holy, holy, holy, God of power and might
35 Holy One, O Holy One
203 *Holy, Holy, Holy* (Kingsfold)
206 *Holy, Holy, Holy* (Patriquin)
15 Holy sacred Spirit
6 Holy Spirit, come into our lives
75 Holy Spirit, come to us
5 Holy Spirit, you're like the wind
148 Hope of Abraham and Sarah
220 Hope shines as the solitary star
95 How deep the peace
29 How lovely is your dwelling place
167 Hush! Hush! Somebody's callin' mah name
157 I am a child of God
201 I am the bread of life
106 I am the dream
221 I am walking a path of peace
48 I can feel you near me God
161 I have called you by your name
108 I know your word, your word is a lamp
61 I praise you, O God
127 I saw the rich ones
188 I thank you, thank you, Jesus
76 If I have been the source of pain, O God
57 I'll praise eternal God
183 I'm gonna shout, shout, shout out my love
181 Imegmoy pitak ay yay
159 In star and crescent, wheel and flame
84 In you there is a refuge
30 It's a song of praise to the Maker
57 Je louerai l'Éternel
189 Jesu tawa pano
33 Jesus came bringing us hope
166 Jesus Christ, Jesus Christ
133 Jesus laughed out loud
210 Jesus, loving Lord
113 Jesus saw them fishing

189 Jesus, we are here
101 Jesus, you fill our hearts
102 Jesus, your Spirit in us
48 *Jump for Joy*
103 Ka mana'o 'I 'O
104 Katonda mulungi
178 *Kindred in Spirit through Jesus Christ*
104 Know that God is good
67 Kyrie eleison (Bridget)
68 Kyrie eleison (Guarani)
69 Kyrie eleison (Kervin)
70 Kyrie eleison (Reindorf)
56 Lajahle, htaora Hp'ya
190 Laughter lit the stars of morning
83 Let my spirit always sing
1 Let us build a house where love can dwell
144 Like a healing stream
98 Like a river of tears
92 Like a rock
97 Listen, God is calling
87 *Living Water*
195 Long ago and far away
63 Long before my journey's start
100 Lord God, you love us
70 Lord, have mercy on us
18 Lord, prepare me to be a sanctuary
181 Lord, your hands have formed
89 Love is the touch of intangible joy
94 Love knocks and waits for us to hear
81 Love us into fullness
19 Maranatha
214 May God's sheltering wings
168 May peace be with you
224 May the God of peace
218 May the love of the Lord
222 May the peace of God
175 May we but wait
151 Mayenziwe 'ntando yakho
118 Me alone
204 *Memorial Acclamation (Kingsfold)*
207 *Memorial Acclamation (Patriquin)*
22 Mi pela i bung
147 *Moments of Myst'ry*
39 Mother Earth, our mother birthing
104 Mungu ni mwema
138 My love colours outside the lines
120 My soul cries out
109 My soul is thirsting for you
224 Na Jijoho
140 Na nzela na lola
129 Naega sanül hyanghayŏ
90 N'ayez pas peur
40 Never ending joy
187 Nous rendons grâce à Dieu

38   Nzamuranza
41   O beautiful Gaia
9   O come, and let us sing
    to God, our hope
68   O God have mercy
25   O God, send out your Spirit
73   O God, why are you silent?
203   O holy, holy, holy God
13   O let the power fall on me
68, 69   Ô Seigneur, prends pitié
70   Ô Seigneur, prends pitié
    de nous
142   Oh, a song must rise
85   Oh! Prends-moi tel que je suis
21   Open our hearts, open
    our minds
68   Oré poriajú verekó Ñandeyara
138   *Outside the Lines*
21   Ouvre nos cœurs
88   Over my head
197   Pain de vie, partagé
202   Pain pour la route
128   *Palm Sunday Processional*
215   Peace be with you
149   Peace for the children
42   Praise God for this holy
    ground
67   Prends pitié, ô Seigneur
31   Pure love
173   Put peace into each other's
    hands
198   Quand nous venons à la table
151   Que ta volonté sois faite
7   Rassemble-nous, tout près
    de toi
187   Reamo leboga
98   *Renewing Our Spirits*
130   *Rise Up, O My Soul*
130   Rise up, rise up, rise up,
    O my soul
3   *River*
160   *River of Life*
163   *River Run Deep*
163   River running in you and me
3   River, rush-a-down to
    the ocean blue
3   Rivière, coule, coule vers
    l'océan
23   Saint-Esprit, viens, oh, viens
168   Salamun, Salamun
18   *Sanctuary*
203   *Sanctus (Kingsfold)*
206   *Sanctus (Patriquin)*
212   Sent out in Jesus' name
66   Senzeni na?
44   Shadow and substance
5   Sheng ling ru feng

183   *Shout Out Your Love*
76   Si fui motivo de dolor, oh Dios
180   *Sing a New Song*
204   Sing, Christ has died
180   Sing, sing out! Sing a
    new song
121   *Singing Hallelujah!*
179   Sisters let us walk together
223   Sizohamba naye
174   Soil of God, you and I
152   *Song of Sanctuary*
55   *Song of Waters*
79   Spirit, open my heart
150   Spirit God, be our breath
99   Stand, O stand firm
85   Take, O take me as I am
213   Take up his song
24   *The Breath, the Word,*
    the Voice
146   The kingdom of God
43   The play of the Godhead
116   The thirsty deer longs for
    the streams
165   There is a time
62   There is room for all
134   There was a child in Galilee
160   There's a river of life
177   This is my body
122   This is the day that God
    has made
176   Three things I promise
129   To the high and kindly hills
100   Toi, tu nous aimes
105   Too'n mera pita
34   Tout est fait pour la gloire
    de Dieu
145   Traçons un grand cercle
139   True faith needs no defence
161   Tu sais je t'ai appelé(e)
    par ton nom
108   Tua palavra é lâmpada
75   *Tui Amoris Ignem*
58   Tuya es la gloria
170   Ubi caritas et amor
155   Unbounded Spirit,
    breath of God
2   Uyai mose
211   Vayan en paz
75   Veni Sancte Spiritus
9   Venite, exultemus Domino
122   Voici le jour que Dieu a fait
71   *Warm the Time of Winter*
55   Watch once more the
    windswept storm clouds
87   Water flowing from
    the mountains
141   We are all one people

143   We cannot own the sunlit sky
192   We come now to your table,
    Lord
187   We give our hands to you
187   We give our thanks to God
58   We sing of your glory
38   We sing your praise/
    Nzamuranza
223   We will go with God
196   We will take what you offer
218   Wei yuan Shen di ai
137   Welcome, Jesus,
    you are welcome
93   What calls me from the death
    where I have rested?
191   What can I do?
125   When a grain of wheat
199   When at this table I receive
    a blessing
136   When hands reach out
    and fingers trace
169   When hands reach out
    beyond divides
74   When painful mem'ries
    haunt each day
71   When the wind of winter
    blows
128   When they heard that Jesus
    was coming
65   When we are tested and
    wrestle alone
198   When we gather at the table
49   When we seek language
170   Where there is charity
14   Where two or three are
    gathered
216   Wherever you may go
178   Who is my mother
72   Why stand so far away
23   *Wind of Change*
127   *Work for a World*
51   Yahweh be praised
210   Yeshu supriya
45   You are holy, you show us
    the way
200   You are my body
105   You are my Father
131   You, Creator God, have
    searched me
152   You who watch the highest
    heavens
26   Your love is amazing, steady
    and unchanging
151   Your will be done